SpringerBriefs in Intelligent Systems

Artificial Intelligence, Multiagent Systems, and Cognitive Robotics

This series covers the entire research and application spectrum of intelligent systems, including artificial intelligence, multiagent systems, and cognitive robotics. Typical texts for publication in the series include, but are not limited to, state-of-the-art reviews, tutorials, summaries, introductions, surveys, and in-depth case and application studies of established or emerging fields and topics in the realm of computational intelligent systems. Essays exploring philosophical and societal issues raised by intelligent systems are also very welcome.

More information about this series at https://link.springer.com/bookseries/11845

Zhongxu Hu · Chen Lv

Vision-Based Human Activity Recognition

 Springer

Zhongxu Hu
School of Mechanical Aerospace
Engineering
Nanyang Technological University
Singapore, Singapore

Chen Lv
School of Mechanical Aerospace
Engineering
Nanyang Technological University
Singapore, Singapore

ISSN 2196-548X   ISSN 2196-5498 (electronic)
SpringerBriefs in Intelligent Systems
ISBN 978-981-19-2289-3   ISBN 978-981-19-2290-9 (eBook)
https://doi.org/10.1007/978-981-19-2290-9

This Springer imprint is published by the registered company Springer Nature Singapore Pte Ltd.
The registered company address is: 152 Beach Road, #21-01/04 Gateway East, Singapore 189721, Singapore

Preface

In recent years, tremendous progress has been made in various intelligent devices and systems, which can be found in many living scenarios and industrial sectors, including smartphones, automated vehicles, and collaborative robots, are now part of our lives, and the proportion will become larger. Therefore, intelligent human–machine interaction which will play an inseparable role has piqued the public's considerable interest, and as a result, numerous advanced interaction methods and interfaces are being investigated to enhance user experience, acceptance, and trust. Visual sensors are now the most widely used ones due to their low-cost, high-quality, and un-intrusive characters, resulting in vision-based human activity recognition (V-HAR) becoming a critical technique for supporting downstream human–machine interaction applications. On the other hand, the deep learning approaches have achieved significant progress in many fields, which also promote V-HAR-related research. As a result, this field is flourished with a multitude of topics and techniques from various perspectives. This book provides a comprehensive overview of the past and current research studies associated with various vision-based approaches focusing on human activity recognition, especially contemporary techniques. It also sheds light on advanced application areas, and futuristic research topics. This book aims to systematically sort out these related tasks and applications and introduce the advanced deep learning methods to help further our understanding of the current state and future potential of the V-HAR research.

There are a total of 6 chapters included in this book. The chapters cover recent vision-based studies for various human activity recognition, including hand pose estimation, hand gesture recognition, head pose estimation, gaze direction estimation, gaze fixation estimation, body pose estimation, human action recognition, body reconstruction, human attention modelling, and other issues. Chapter 1 gives an overview of human activity recognition research, which introduces the background and the taxonomy of the related topics for the V-HAR. Chapter 2 focuses on the vision-based hand activity recognition, which firstly introduces the depth sensor-based hand pose estimation leveraging the deep learning approach and presents the optimization solutions from the multi-scale feature fusion and the multi-frame complementary perspectives, then an efficient dynamic hand gesture recognition approach is discussed. Chapter 3 presents the vision-based facial activity recognition approaches, where an end-to-end head pose estimation model is firstly introduced, then a dynamic head tracking system is presented; furthermore, the appearance-based gaze direction and fixation estimation solutions are also introduced. Chapter 4 discusses vision-based body activity recognition, which includes body pose estimation, action recognition, and reconstruction. The corresponding state-of-the-art methods are reviewed and summarized. Chapter 5 introduces human attention modelling, where a context-aware approach is presented to couple with the visual saliency information of the scenarios. The conclusions and the recommendations for the V-HAR are presented in Chap. 6.

As a professional reference and research monograph, this book covers multiple popular research topics and includes cross-domain knowledge, which will benefit readers from various levels of expertise in broad fields of science and engineering, including professional researchers, graduate students, university faculties, etc. This book will help the readers to systematically study the related topics and give an overview of this field.

The completion of this book owes to not only the work of the authors but also many other individuals and groups. Special thanks would first go to all our group members of Automated Driving and Human–Machine System (AutoMan) Lab, especially Peng Hang, Yang Xing, Chao Huang, Xiangkun He, Shanhe Lou, Hao Chen, Jingda Wu, Yiran Zhang, Yanxin Zhou, Xiaoyu Mo, Tianchu Su, Wenhui Huang, and Haohan Yang, for their generous assistance. We are grateful to all members of the Rehabilitation Research Institute of Singapore (RRIS) and the Continental-NTU Corporate Lab, Nanyang Technological University, for the constant feedback and support to this work. Then, we thank Jingying Chen and Sivananth Siva Chandran in the publication team at Springer for their assistance. Finally, sincere thanks to our beloved families for their consideration as well as encouragement.

Research efforts summarized in this book were supported in part by the A*STAR Grant (No. W1925d0046) of Singapore, National Key Research, in part by the Alibaba Innovative Research Program and the Alibaba–Nanyang Technological University Joint Research Institute (No. AN-GC-2020-012), and in part by the RIE2020 Industry Alignment Fund–Industry Collaboration Projects (IAF-ICP) Funding Initiative, as well as cash and in-kind contributions from the industry partner(s).

Singapore   Zhongxu Hu
March 2022

Contents

Acronyms

2D	Two-Dimensional
3D	Three-Dimensional
AI	Artificial Intelligence
AKF	Adaptive Kalman Filter
AR	Augmented Reality
BDD-A	Berkeley Deep Drive Attention
BP	Back Propagation
CC	Correlation Coefficient
CNN	Convolutional Neural Network
CRF	Conditional Random Field
CRNN	Convolutional Recurrent Neural Network
DC	Deep Convolutional Neural Network
DL	Deep Learning
DT	Decision Tree
ECG	Electrocardiogram
EEG	Electroencephalogram
EMG	Electromyography
ERF	Effective Receptive Field
GAN	Generative Adversarial Network
GNN	Graph Neural Network
HAR	Human Activity Recognition
HCI	Human Computer Interaction
HCPS	Human–Cyber–Physical System
HOG	Histograms-Oriented Gradients
HRNet	High-Resolution Representation Network
IG	Information Gain
IMU	Inertial Measurement Unit
IR	Infrared
KD	K-Dimensional
KF	Kalman Filter
KL	Kullback–Leibler

KNN	K-Nearest Neighbors
LSH	Locality Sensitive Hashing
LSTM	Long Short-Term Memory
MAE	Mean Absolute Error
MHI	Motion History Image
MLP	Multi-Layer Perceptron
MRF	Markov Random Fields
MSE	Mean Square Error
NAS	Neural Architecture Search
NeRF	Neural Radiance Field
NLP	Natural Language Processing
NN	Neural Network
NNb	Nearest Neighbor
NSFC	National Natural Science Foundation of China
NSS	Normalized Scanpath Saliency
NYU	New York University
PIFu	Pixel-aligned Implicit Function
ReLU	Rectified Linear Unit
RF	Random Forest
RGB	Red-Green-Blue
RGB-D	RGB-Depth
RNN	Recurrent Neural Network
RPN	Region Proposal Network
SAE	Society of Automotive Engineers
SIFT	Scale-Invariant Feature Transform
SMPL	Skinned Multi-Person Linear
SSC	Similarity Sensitive Coding
ST-ViT	Spatial-Temporal Vision Transformer
SURF	Speed Up Robust Features
SVM	Support Vector Machine
SVR	Support Vector Regression
T-ViT	Temporal Vision Transformer
V-HAR	Vision-based Human Activity Recognition
VR	Virtual Reality
WoS	Web of Science

Chapter 1
Introduction

Abstract This chapter gives an overview of human activity recognition as well as its commonly used sensors. We start from the background and challenges in vision-based human activity recognition. Then the related specific tasks are sorted out and the general solutions are briefly introduced. The instantiated tasks to be elaborated in the following chapters are finally discussed in a compact manner.

1.1 Background of Human Activity Recognition

In recent years, tremendous progress has been made in advanced sensing and intelligent method, which has promoted the deployment of intelligent systems in many living scenarios and industrial sectors. The intelligent agents, including smartphone, intelligent vehicles, and robots, are now part of our lives, and the proportion will become larger. On the other hand, the coexisting and collaboration of humans and machines have been a broad consensus in many fields. The National Natural Science Foundation of China (NSFC) recently announced the launch of the Tri-Co Robot (Coexisting-Cooperative-Cognitive Robot) major research program. It aims to ensure that robotics technology is ubiquitous for the enhancement of human life and work in an inherently safe manner, allow robots to effectively collaborate and coordinate with humans, and emphasize robots' abilities to perceive and predict the behaviour and intent of humans [1]. With the development of information technology, intelligent manufacturing has progressed through the stages of digital manufacturing and digital-networked manufacturing and is now evolving towards new-generation intelligent manufacturing, which is characterized by the in-depth integration of new-generation artificial intelligence (AI) technology. Zhou et al. [2] proposed the human–cyber–physical system (HCPS), which is a composite intelligent system composed of humans, cyber systems, and physical systems with the goal of optimizing specific manufacturing goals. The Society of Automotive Engineers (SAE) International [3] provided a clarify taxonomy with detailed definitions for six levels of driving automation, ranging from no driving automation (Level 0) to full driving automation (Level 5). This standard report indicates that the human and automated vehicle will coexist

Z. Hu and C. Lv, *Vision-Based Human Activity Recognition*,
SpringerBriefs in Intelligent Systems,
https://doi.org/10.1007/978-981-19-2290-9_1

Fig. 1.1 The HAR is an important enabling technology to support the complete human–machine system

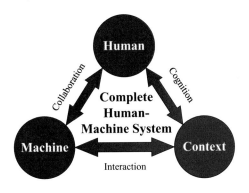

for a long period, and it requires a mutual understanding between the human and vehicle. Facebook Horizon, a social virtual reality (VR) world, was launched in 2019 by the well-known social network company Facebook, and was then renamed "Meta Platforms," and its chairman declared a "metaverse" concept in 2021 [4]. It depicts a virtual world where the human can have a virtual replica created using interactions and biometric data from wearable virtual reality devices.

The preceding introductions have provided a brief overview of cutting-edge technology in various fields, and we can see that these technologies rely on intelligent human–machine systems, as shown in Fig. 1.1, to support context awareness, perception and cognitive abilities, personalization, and adaptation. They emphasize the importance of human–machine collaboration and have spawned a new wave of intelligent human–machine systems. Therefore, the smartness, safety, and efficiency of the interactions and collaborations between humans and intelligent agents should be further explored by leveraging advanced intelligent algorithms.

Understanding human activities is a critical task for constructing a harmonious human–machine system because they provide critical information at multiple levels of human conditions, which could be utilized in many scenarios, including smartphones, multimedia entertainment, security monitoring, healthcare, autonomous vehicle, intelligent living, human–computer interaction, to name a few. As a result, it has attracted numerous attentions from various fields. We have searched it with the keyword "human activity recognition (HAR)" in the Web of Science (WoS) [5], and the search results are shown in Fig. 1.2. It can be clearly found that the relevant publications have gradually increased over the past two decades, which demonstrate that HAR is a promising and hot research topic. This also benefits from the development of the AI technology represented by the deep learning (DL) [6–8], which promotes numerous researchers of various fields to revisit this topic from a variety of perspective.

Despite significant progress has been made in HAR, there are still several major challenges in this task. The first is the diversity and complexity of the human, which results in the significant variations of the same activity being widespread across the relevant tasks. It could degrade the utilized algorithms and increase the difficulty in

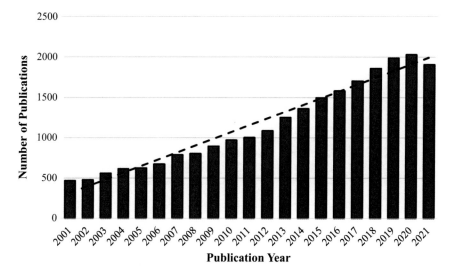

Fig. 1.2 The number of publications on human activity recognition published over the last two decades based on the WoS search engine

recognition, which requires that the individual behaviour pattern should be considered to avoid misclassification. This also elicits the second challenge of lack of a large amount of dataset. The current advanced methods basically adopt a data-driven approach, in which the robustness and accuracy of them highly rely on the scale of training set. A lot of existing studies have shown impressive performance on the small dataset with limited activity classes or in the laboratory environment, however, the recognition in the large and realistic dataset is still a challenging task. This will affect the generalization of the developed models. In addition, the complex environment and background noise could increase the difficulty of the recognition, especially for the camera sensors that are sensitive to the illumination conditions, viewpoint transformations, dynamic scenarios, and so on. Due to the existing challenges, the HAR has attracted increasing researchers to make effort to optimize it for various applications.

1.2 Commonly Used Sensor Types

The concept of the HAR in this book involves various kinds of activities, including static pose and gesture, dynamic behaviour, attention & intention state, physiological state, and personality. Meanwhile, various multi-modal sensors are explored for various applications in the past decades [9, 10]. In our opinion, the activities can literally be divided into two categories: internal and external, as shown as in Fig. 1.3. The internal activities mainly include the physiological and psychological ones, and

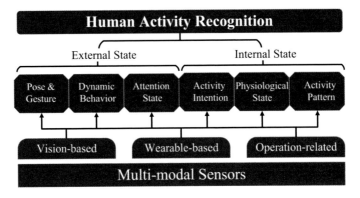

Fig. 1.3 The taxonomy of the HAR and its commonly used sensors

they basically rely on specific wearable sensors to identify [11, 12], such as Electromyography (EMG), Electroencephalogram (EEG), Electrocardiogram (ECG), etc. In practice, some additional sensors, like operation-related and appearance-related, are also required to supplement the recognition of the internal activity [13]. The wearable sensors can provide robust perception for the specific condition, so they are also often utilized for external activity recognition, such as the data gloves and motion capture suit. However, these wearable sensors are usually expensive, which is not conducive to widespread applications. Furthermore, the intrusive usage also reduces the acceptance and experience of the end-user. Therefore, the non-intrusive visual sensors have attracted numerous attentions and have been deployed in various intelligent devices and systems due to its affordable and portable. The advancement of computer vision technology has promoted its progress further.

1.3 Taxonomy of Vision-Based Human Activity Recognition

The vision-based sensor is now the most widely used sensor and ubiquitous due to its low-cost, high-quality, and un-intrusive characteristics. As a result, an increasing number of related researchers are paying attention to it and leveraging it to tackle the HAR task. The rapid development of computer vision and intelligent perception technology also contributes to its popularity. This book will also focus on the vision-based HAR(V-HAR) and introduce the emerging technologies on V-HAR, especially the DL-based approach. The DL-based approaches have achieved significant progress, which inspired considerable research topics for the V-HAR in various applications. However, there is no suitable book that covers these topics and clearly explains the inter- and intra-relationship between these topics, especially using the emerging deep learning model. This book aims to systematically sort out these related tasks and applications and introduce the advanced deep learning models used on it.

As above stated, the V-HAR primarily focuses on external activities by recognizing appearance-based behaviour, but it can also be utilized to infer the internal state due to the interconnectedness of the various human states. The related research topics from literately view can be classified into three broad categories: hand-related, facial-related, and body-related, as shown in Fig. 1.4. The hand-related topics include the two-dimensional (2D) & three-dimensional (3D) hand pose estimation, static hand gesture recognition, and dynamic hand gesture recognition. Hand-related recognition has been widely deployed to many applications due to its natural interaction manner, such as virtual/augmented reality (V/AR) interaction, smart cockpit control, contactless interaction of the smartphone, to name a few. Similarly, the body-related topics include 2D & 3D body pose estimation, human body action recognition, body reconstruction, and other behaviour tracking and analysis tasks. The body-related recognition is mainly utilized for large-scale interaction scenarios, including smart dressing mirrors, interactive entertainment, collaborative robotics, intelligent manufacturing, and public security, amongst others. In comparison, the facial-related topics are more sophisticated, which mainly consist of facial recognition, head pose estimation, and eye gaze perception. At present, face recognition technology is very mature, and it is adopted in many daily applications as an important identification method, and it will not be repeated in this book. The head pose is indispensable data to improve the immersion of the VR system and is also commonly utilized to infer the distraction state of the human. The eye gaze task includes gaze direction estimation and fixation estimation, which is an important clue to understanding human attention. Due to the facial features being more directly related to the mental state, they are also utilized in affective computing and intention prediction tasks.

The commonly used vision-based sensors can be categorized into three types: red–green–blue (RGB), depth, and infrared. The RGB sensor is the most widely used one due to its high-quality sensing and low-cost characteristics, and it is more aligned with the human perception of colours. Therefore, it has been extensively equipped with electronic systems, such as digital cameras, televisions, computers,

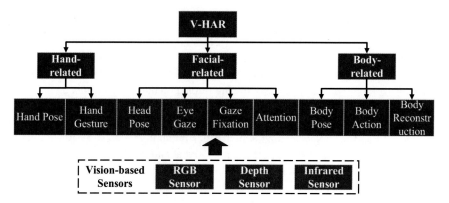

Fig. 1.4 The taxonomy of the V-HAR related topics and related vision-based sensors

Fig. 1.5 The general pipeline of the V-HAR tasks

mobile phones, video projectors, and image scanners, to name a few, resulting in the largest and most widely RGB image dataset. However, the disadvantage of the RGB sensor is only capturing the 2D colour matric data which is not conducive to the understanding of the 3D information of the real world. Although the computer vision geometry technology can be leveraged to overcome this limitation, it is still not as effective as obtaining depth information directly from the depth sensor. Therefore, the depth sensor is commonly adopted in 3D information-related applications, such as 3D hand pose estimation, 3D body pose estimation, head pose estimation, amongst others. However, the limitation of depth sensor is its low resolution and low-quality output, which is more common in commercial devices. As a result, many studies usually combine it with the RGB sensor to recognize human activities in tandem. Furthermore, the infrared sensor is also utilized to outcome the poor illumination conditions, where the RGB sensor cannot work well. It is common to be deployed in the smart cockpit of the intelligent vehicle which needs to tackle the diverse illumination conditions and the driver with eyeglasses. Each of these sensors has advantages and disadvantages, and the researchers can adopt appropriate configurations according to the specific application.

From the methodology perspective, the general pipeline of the V-HAR task consists of the vision-based input capture, the pre-processing, the feature extraction, the classification/regression, and the final recognition output, as illustrated in Fig. 1.5. The input basically is the matric data with multiple channels according to the used sensor, such as 3 channels for the RGB image and 1 channel for the depth image. Typically, pre-processing is required by leveraging image processing technology to reduce white noise, enhance image quality, normalize the image, or segment the region of interest, etc. For example, the hand and head area can be detected to achieve the robust recognition of their related tasks. In addition, background subtraction and tracking are popular methods for recognizing dynamic activity with the static viewpoint, whereas optical flow and temporal difference are used to detect moving objects for the non-static viewpoint. The feature extraction is the most important stage of the pipeline, and it has a significant impact on the recognition's final performance. It can be classified into two approaches: handcrafted feature-based methods and deep feature-based methods. The traditional pattern recognition approach is the handcrafted feature-based method, which relies on an ingeniously designed feature descriptor based on some rules. Many classic global and local feature descriptors are proposed, which have rotation and scale-invariant under various illuminations and occlusion, such as the scale-invariant feature transform (SIFT) [14], speed up robust features (SURF) [15], and histograms-oriented gradients (HOG) [16]. These features are extracted for the activity representation from the perspectives of shape, colour, contour, motion, silhouette, and so on. The performance of recognition will be heavily influenced by the representation quality of them in capturing human-specific activity and spatial–temporal changes. Therefore, there are a lot of studies that make effort to improve the representation capability from various perspectives. Once the representation features being extracted, the classification or regression algorithms are applied for recognizing the specific activity. The classic classification approaches, as known as the discriminative model, include linear regression [17], logistic regression [18], support vector machine (SVM) [19], conditional random field (CRF) [20], Gaussian process [21], to name a few. The regression methods have K-nearest neighbors (KNN) [22], Gaussian mixture model [23], hidden Markov models [24], dynamic Bayesian networks [25], Markov random fields (MRF) [26], artificial neural network [27], amongst others. These typical algorithms have promoted the advancement of V-HAR in a variety of applications; however, these methods are not suitable for handling a large number of activity samples, which will limit the model performance and make it difficult to be improved in a data-driven way.

The DL-based methods have achieved tremendous success in a variety of fields in the domain of computer vision in recent years, and the V-HAR tasks are no exception. There have been numerous outstanding works on the V-HAR that make use of deep networks. Compared with the traditional approach, the DL-based method can let the model learn the feature extraction in a data-driven manner without a handcrafted one. Furthermore, the traditional handcrafted feature can be considered as the fixed shallow model. In comparison, the DL-based method can increase the complexity of the model, where the learning capability of the machine learning models is positively correlated with the model complexity. The non-linear embedding, on the other hand, is enhanced by increasing the model depth. In addition, the DL method can extract the multi-levels of representations, where the input image is increasingly abstracted from the low-level of pixel and silhouette to the high-level part. Overall, the DL-based method can obtain a better representation and increase the model robustness to the various conditions in a data-driven manner. The difference between the traditional approach and the DL-based one can be summarized as illustrated in Fig. 1.6.

Due to the vision-based input is basically metric format data, the convolutional neural network (CNN) is the most used DL-based module for V-HAR. The reason for this is that the CNN has outstanding properties that enable invariance to the affine transformations of the fed feature maps, allowing it to recognize patterns that are translation, rotation, and slightly warped within the feature maps. The local receptive field, shared weight, and spatial pooling are the key enabling characteristics of the CNN. The local receptive field enables the CNN to learn low-level features in the lower layers, such as lines, edges, contours, and so on. Whilst high-level abstract features such as shape can be learned in higher layers, since the image area exposed by units in higher layers is larger due to spatial pooling that makes the accumulated receptive field of previous lower layers larger. This concept of local receptive field is also inspired by the biological structure of the visual system, in which neurons in the visual cortex only respond to stimuli in specific regions. The weights required by the convolutional neural network are further reduced by further sharing the weights.

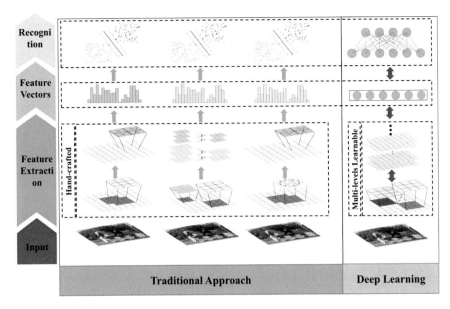

Fig. 1.6 The comparison of the traditional approach and the deep learning-based one

Second, using the pooling operation gives the network a certain degree of translation invariance and can also give the network a larger receptive field layer by layer.

To tackle the sequential input in some applications, the recurrent neural network (RNN) [28], long short-term memory (LSTM) [29] and 3D CNN model [30], that can capture the temporal structure of the activity. The RNN is a typical neural network that can handle sequential or time series data for sequential or temporal tasks like human action recognition and dynamic hand gesture recognition. They are distinguished by their "memory," which allows them to influence the current input and output by using information from previous ones. Unlike traditional deep neural networks, which assume that inputs and outputs are independent of one another, the output of RNN is dependent on the preceding elements in the sequence. Another distinguishing characteristic of the RNN is that it can share parameters across all network layers. Unlike the classic feedforward networks, which have different weights for each node, the RNN has the same weight parameter shared by each layer of the network. However, these weights are still learnable in the backpropagation and gradient descent processes to facilitate reinforcement learning. The RNN, on the other hand, frequently encounters two issues: exploding gradients and vanishing gradients. The size of the gradient, which is the slope of the loss function along the error curve, defines these issues. When the gradient is too small, it continues to shrink, updating the weight parameters until they become insignificant. When this happens, the learning of the neural network model would stop. When a gradient becomes too large, it explodes, resulting in an unstable model. One approach to addressing these issues is to reduce the number of hidden layers, thereby removing some of the complexity in the RNN model. The LSTM is a more advanced RNN model that allows information to be persisted, and which can solve the vanishing gradient problem that RNN has. They, like RNNs, remember previous information and use it to process the current input. However, RNNs have a shortcoming in that they cannot remember long-term dependencies due to the vanishing gradient, this problem is explicitly avoided by LSTMs. By enforcing constant error flow through constant error carousels within special units and truncating the gradient where it does not harm, LSTM can learn to bridge minimal time lags in excess of 1000 discrete-time steps. Access to the constant error flow is opened and closed by multiplicative gate units. The 3D CNN is another approach to handle the sequential data by extension the typical 2D CNN in the temporal dimension. The kernel in 2D CNN moves in two directions. The input and output data of a 2D CNN are three-dimensional, which is commonly used on image data. The kernel in 3D CNN moves in three directions, and the input and output data of 3D CNN are four dimensional. The 3D CNN, in comparison to the RNN and LSTM, is more focused on learning temporally local features.

Leveraging the basic neural network modules, the different neural networks with various types of combinations can be constructed according to the specific application. By utilizing the benefits of the pre-training approach, many works can achieve outstanding performance when compared to other state-of-the-art methods. Besides the commonly used single stream structure, some studies adopted the multiple stream architecture to handle the multi-model input, such as the RGB image and depth map. In addition, the multi-stream architecture is also common to tackle the motion feature map, such as the optical flow and frame differences map that can highlight the motion area, whereas the main branch is trained to handle the raw frames. The extracted feature maps from the different branches are concatenated and fused before being fed into the final recognition module, which results in the final combined decision. Another class of traditional approaches to activity recognition employs a combination of LSTM and CNN. These methods consider the CNN module as the feature extractor and the extracted features are fed into the LSTM module to capture the change of the activities in features from each frame.

The challenges of the V-HAR can be summarized as follows: low image quality, variable illumination, high-speed activity, occlusion, dynamic viewpoint, indefinite inter- and intra-class variance, person diversity, spatial–temporal scale variation, and recording settings variation. The first five issues are the common challenges of the vision-based tasks due to the visual sensor being sensitive to the change in environmental conditions. The other challenges further increase the difficulty of the recognition. These necessitate that the developed models have the intelligence to tackle the task in a robust manner.

1.4 Summary

A comprehensive introduction of the V-HAR is presented in the above sections. The V-HAR, a fundamental technology for constructing harmonious human–machine systems in various industrial and real-life domains, has recently become a hot and vibrant research topic to increase the intelligence, efficiency, and safety of interactions and collaborations. The goal of this book is to provide an overview of its various aspects in order to systematically sort out these related topics and applications, as well as to introduce the advanced deep learning models that were used on it. For the involved tasks, the benchmark and state-of-the-art method will be thoroughly explored and discussed. Finally, based on current constraints and challenges, we will recommend some future research directions. We hope that this book will inspire new research efforts and serve as a comprehensive review document for this field.

This chapter is organized as follows. We will describe the related studies one by one, including vision-based hand activity recognition, vision-based facial-related activity recognition, vision-based body activity recognition, and vision-based human attention modelling. Each case study follows the same format: an introduction and background review, the involved sub-topic, the typical method or model, and finally analysis. The chapter is then concluded with a discussion of the limitations and future work.

References

1. Ding H, Yang X, Zheng N, Li M, Lai Y, Wu H (2018) Tri-co robot: a Chinese robotic research initiative for enhanced robot interaction capabilities. Natl Sci Rev 5(6):799–801
2. Zhou J, Zhou Y, Wang B, Zang J (2019) Human–cyber–physical systems (HCPSs) in the context of new-generation intelligent manufacturing. Engineering 5(4):624–636
3. Committee SO-RAVS et al (2014) Taxonomy and definitions for terms related to on-road motor vehicle automated driving systems. SAE Standard J 3016:1–16
4. Stokel-Walker C (2022) Welcome to the metaverse. New Sci 253(3368):39–43
5. Clarivate. Web of science. https://www.webofscience.com/wos/woscc/basic-search
6. Hu Z-X, Wang Y, Ge M-F, Liu J (2020) Data-driven fault diagnosis method based on compressed sensing and improved multiscale network. IEEE Trans Ind Electron 67(4):3216–3225
7. Liu J, Hu Y, Wang Y, Wu B, Fan J, Hu Z (2018) An integrated multi-sensor fusion-based deep feature learning approach for rotating machinery diagnosis. Measure Sci Technol 29(5):055103
8. Zhou K, Yang C, Liu J, Xu Q (2021) Dynamic graph-based feature learning with few edges considering noisy samples for rotating machinery fault diagnosis. IEEE Trans Ind Electron 1–1. https://doi.org/10.1109/TIE.2021.3121748
9. Jha S, Marzban MF, Hu T, Mahmoud MH, Al-Dhahir N, Busso C (2021) The multimodal driver monitoring database: a naturalistic corpus to study driver attention. IEEE Trans Intell Transp Syst 1–17
10. Marcano M, Daz S, Prez J, Irigoyen E (2020) A review of shared control for automated vehicles: Theory and applications. IEEE Trans Hum-Mach Syst 50(6):475–491
11. Zhang C, Eskandarian A (2021) A survey and tutorial of eeg-based brain monitoring for driver state analysis. IEEE/CAA J Automatica Sinica 8(7):1222–1242
12. Katsigiannis S, Ramzan N (2017) Dreamer: a database for emotion recognition through eeg and ecg signals from wireless low-cost off-the-shelf devices. IEEE J Biomed Health Inform 22(1):98–107
13. Nmcov A, Svozilov V, Bucsuhzy K, Smek R, Mzl M, Hesko B, Belk M, Bilk M, Maxera P, Seitl M, Dominik T, Semela M, Ucha M, Kol R (2021) Multimodal features for detection of driver stress and fatigue: review. IEEE Trans Intell Transp Syst 22(6):3214–3233

14. Lowe DG (1999) Object recognition from local scale-invariant features. In: Proceedings of the seventh IEEE international conference on computer vision, vol 2. IEEE, pp 1150–1157
15. Bay H, Tuytelaars T, Gool LV (2006) Surf: speeded up robust features. In: European conference on computer vision. Springer, pp 404–417
16. Dalal N, Triggs B (2005) Histograms of oriented gradients for human detection. In: 2005 IEEE Computer society conference on computer vision and pattern recognition (CVPR'05), vol 1. IEEE, pp 886–893
17. Naseem I, Togneri R, Bennamoun M (2010) Linear regression for face recognition. IEEE Trans Pattern Anal Mach Intell 32(11):2106–2112
18. Peng C-YJ, Lee KL, Ingersoll GM (2002) An introduction to logistic regression analysis and reporting. J Educ Res 96(1):3–14
19. Noble WS (2006) What is a support vector machine? Nat Biotechnol 24(12):1565–1567
20. Sutton C, McCallum A (2006) An introduction to conditional random fields for relational learning. Introduction Stat Relat Learn 2:93–128
21. Wang JM, Fleet DJ, Hertzmann A (2007) Gaussian process dynamical models for human motion. IEEE Trans Pattern Anal Mach Intell 30(2):283–298
22. Keller JM, Gray MR, Givens JA (1985) A fuzzy k-nearest neighbor algorithm. IEEE Trans Syst Man Cybern 4:580–585
23. Rasmussen C (1999) The infinite Gaussian mixture model. In: Advances in neural information processing systems, vol 12
24. Eddy SR (2004) What is a hidden markov model? Nat Biotechnol 22(10):1315–1316
25. Ghahramani Z (1997) Learning dynamic Bayesian networks. In: International school on neural networks, initiated by IIASS and EMFCSC. Springer, pp 168–197
26. Boykov Y, Veksler O, Zabih R (1998) Markov random fields with efficient approximations. In: Proceedings. 1998 IEEE computer society conference on computer vision and pattern recognition (Cat. No. 98CB36231). IEEE, pp 648–655
27. Hopfield JJ (1988) Artificial neural networks. IEEE Circ Devices Mag 4(5):3–10
28. Mikolov T, Karafiát M, Burget L, Cernocký, J, Khudanpur S (2010) Recurrent neural network based language model. In: Interspeech, vol 2. Makuhari, pp1045–1048
29. Hochreiter S, Schmidhuber J (1997) Long short-term memory. Neural Comput 9(8):1735–1780
30. Ji S, Xu W, Yang M, Yu K (2012) 3d convolutional neural networks for human action recognition. IEEE Trans Pattern Anal Mach Intell 35(1):221–231

Chapter 2
Vision-Based Hand Activity Recognition

Abstract This chapter focuses on the hand activity recognition topics, including hand pose estimation, the static and dynamic hand gesture recognition. The research background is reviewed, and the various approaches have been surveyed and sorted out. Basically, deep learning-based methods are the mainstream solution capable of achieving state-of-the-art performance. This chapter presents the commonly used depth sensor-based approaches for the hand pose estimation firstly, as well as several typical deep learning-based models leveraging the multi-scale spatial information and the multi-frames temporal information. This chapter also introduces a reasonable solution to tackle dynamic hand gesture recognition, which aims to reduce the computational cost to meet the practical needs. In the last, we discuss the unsettled issues and provide some recommendations.

2.1 Introduction

Hand activity recognition is an important task of human–computer interaction research, and it is divided into three categories of study: static gestures, dynamic gestures, and hand pose estimation. Static gesture recognition primarily identifies the fixed gesture state, focusing on hand posture in a single frame state, as shown in the left of Fig. 2.1. The dynamic gesture recognition refers to the identification of continuously changing gesture sequences, which increases when compared to static gestures. It considers the gesture state in the time dimension, as shown in the middle of Fig. 2.1. The hand pose estimation refers to the real-time estimation of the gesture pose, as shown in the right of Fig. 2.1.

When the gesture posture parameters in a specific state are considered as a high-dimensional vector, the gesture posture parameters in all states can form a high-dimensional state space, as shown in Fig. 2.2, where f_t refers to classifying a frame at time t. Static and dynamic gestures only need to classify these data roughly, whereas gesture estimation requires estimating the value of each point, which can also be used to classify the data more finely, making it more difficult.

Z. Hu and C. Lv, *Vision-Based Human Activity Recognition*,
SpringerBriefs in Intelligent Systems,
https://doi.org/10.1007/978-981-19-2290-9_2

Fig. 2.1 The taxonomy of the hand gesture recognition, static gesture, dynamic gesture, hand pose, from left to right

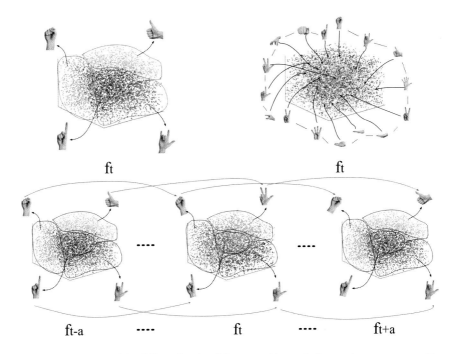

Fig. 2.2 Illustrations of the different hand activity recognition tasks in a vector space perspective

From the standpoint of the sensor, hand gesture recognition can be divided into three categories: data glove, 2D image, and depth image. Data gloves are relatively reliable, but they are inconvenient to use due to the requirement to wear corresponding peripherals, so more researchers prefer image-based methods; and because two-dimensional images lack depth information, the robustness of the model is often poor; in recent years, with the rise of consumer-grade depth cameras, such as Kinect, RealSense, and so on, the research is primarily based on depth images. When compared to two-dimensional images, it can obtain depth information about

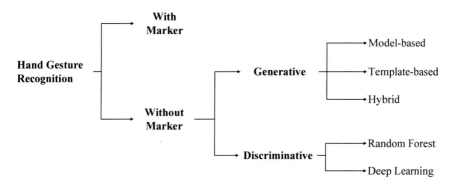

Fig. 2.3 The taxonomy of the hand gesture recognition approaches

the target, which can improve model accuracy, so it has piqued the interest of many researchers.

Due to the high flexibility of the hand and the problem of hand self-occlusion, it is still difficult to completely and accurately recover the full degree of freedom hand pose from the colour map and the depth map, so it has piqued the interest of many researchers. Existing research methods can be classified into two types: with marker and without marker, as illustrated in Fig. 2.3. The following sections go over these methods, with a focus on the latter.

2.1.1 Hand Recognition with Marker

Due to the similar colour and lack of distinct edges of the hand parts when free handing, one approach is to use colour markers to distinguish the parts of the hand, as shown in Fig. 2.4. Chua et al. [1] adopted a series of markers of different colours

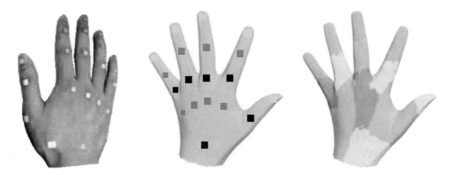

Fig. 2.4 The most common approaches with the marker. reflective marker (left), various colour marker (middle), and colour Gloves (right)

distributed on keypoints of the hand, such as fingertips and wrists, in order to detect changes in hand pose. A 3D hand model with 27 pose parameters is used to fit the 2D positions of these landmarks on the image. To reduce the complexity, the 27 pose parameters are reduced to 20 by analysing the constraints of hand movement. Finally, the hand pose estimation is achieved under the constraints of hand movement through the inverse dynamic solver and these keypoint parameters. Theobalt et al. [2] placed 18 markers with 4 colours on the hand joint points for tracking hand movements. In order to achieve stable extraction, the number of colours used for markers was limited, and the distance between markers of the same colour was the largest. In this way, different joint points can be better identified. Wang et al. [3] used a colour glove to segment the hand area. The glove contains twenty colour blocks with a total of 10 colours, so that different colour blocks can be segmented more stably. By establishing a template data set, the hand rotation and joint point coordinates are estimated and recognized by template matching. Amongst them, the Harsdorf-like distance measurement method is used as the similarity judgement standard, and the similarity sensitive coding (SSC) is used to index the data set to improve the nearest neighbour search efficiency, and then the result of fusion of the most similar templates found is used as the final gesture. Zhao et al. [4] distributed twenty reflective markers on the joint points of the hand and used the Vicon camera acquisition system to obtain the three-dimensional coordinates of these marker points. Although these landmarks cannot be identified and corresponded at runtime, they still provide strong constraints and narrow the search space, thereby improving the accuracy of gesture estimation.

2.1.2 Hand Recognition Without Marker

There are two main types of recognition methods without marker: generative methods and discriminative methods. Let the input data collected by the sensor be x, and the hand pose parameter to be estimated is θ. The generative method often considers the joint probability distribution $y \sim p(x, \theta)$ between the two, or measures the input data x and θ. The similarity relationship between the hand parameters θ to be output; whilst the discriminant method solves the mapping relationship between the input x and the output θ, that is, $y \sim p(\theta|x)$.

1. Generative Approach
There are generally two approaches to generative methods: model-based and template-based, and both have many applications. The model-based method generally uses the model to continuously fit the input image in a controlled environment to obtain continuous estimation results sensitive. In comparison, the template-based method is faster and more robust to initialization but requires a large amount of training data and lacks good discrimination and retrieval capabilities for similar poses. A large number of samples are generated, and the hand pose parameters belong to a high-dimensional space, so a sufficiently dense sampling set cannot be obtained, resulting in the template-based method often obtaining discrete prediction

results. On the other hand, these two methods can also be combined to make up for each other's shortcomings. For example, the template-based method can be used in the initialization stage of the model-based method, or the model-based method can be used for several candidate optimal search for the solution.

Model-based methods generally use the established deformable hand model to iteratively adjust the parameters of the hand model to fit the input image to find the optimal solution. To this end, the hand model must be similar to the shape of the hand and has enough space for hand parameter transformation. Therefore, the design and selection of a suitable hand model is very important. In addition, the calculation speed of model-based related operations is fast, such as model update, model projection calculation, model feature extraction, etc., which can make the input image fully and effectively matched. At the same time, for any gesture, the hand model needs to maintain enough similar details with the real hand. This is actually two seemingly contradictory requirements, that is, the more details, the more computing power will be required, and vice versa. In many cases, a balance needs to be made according to the actual application environment. For example, for some later animation synthesis, real-time estimation is not required, and more emphasis can be placed on model details. In this case, realistic hand with skin and complete joint bones is generally used. However, more gesture-based human–computer interaction needs to be able to achieve real time, so it is more inclined to emphasize the related operation of the model that can be implemented faster. In this case, a simplified version of the hand model is often used, such as consisting of basic voxels such as quadric surfaces. Recently, Gaussian models have also been used for hand and human pose fitting, mainly by attaching a series of Gaussian models to kinematic bones for fitting hands and human surfaces. Compared with geometric models, this method is more efficient in solving the gradient of the objective function. It is easier to analyse and improve the optimization efficiency.

In general, with a suitable hand model, the matching error is estimated by establishing the correspondence between the model and the input image. The typical hand models include the fine-grained mesh surface model [5], approximate quadric model [6], approximate spherical model [7], and Gaussian fitting model [8]. According to some error metric, model-based methods often need to establish an objective function to minimize this error. Generally, some pose parameters are selected or randomly estimated at first, and then updated iteratively until a certain termination criterion is satisfied. Wu and Huang [9] decoupled hand pose parameters into global motion as well as local finger joints and estimated them separately. The gesture pose is assumed to be fixed in the global motion estimation, and the fingertip is used as an end-effector to estimate the local finger motion using inverse dynamics. Affected by fingertip extraction and self-occlusion, this method is less robust. Stenger et al. [10] used quadric surfaces to model hand contours for matching with figure contours. Lin et al. [11] constructed a discrete hand pose parameter space and indexed it with a K-dimensional (KD) tree and used the Nelder–Mead algorithm to search for the parametric solution most similar to the edges and silhouettes of the input image. Felzenszwalb and Huttenlocher [12] constructed the human body as a deformable illustrated structure in which the connections between the two body parts are approximated as spring connections. The pose estimation is achieved by minimizing the matching error between the model and the input image and the energy of the pairwise connections of the parts, which are then efficiently solved using the generalized distance transform. Ueda et al. [13] used cameras from multiple angles to capture hand images and extracted multiple hand silhouettes, in which a blue panel was used as the background to facilitate hand segmentation. The voxel model is obtained by matching the multi-angle image data with the 3D hand model, and then the pose parameters are optimized by keeping the surface of the hand model in the voxel model. de La Gorce et al. [14] obtained hand skin textures and shadows from input images and synthesized them in the hand model, controlled the illumination source in the real scene and simulated it during modelling, and proposed a variational formula for estimating full the degree of freedom hand pose greatly reduces the fuzzy matching, which greatly improves the restoration accuracy of the hand pose. However, this method is often difficult to use in real human–computer interaction scenarios. Oikonomidis et al. [15] used the Kinect depth camera to acquire hand images, which effectively alleviated the problems of background clutter and pose blur in monocular colour images. The 3D hand model parameters that best fit the input depth map and skin colour silhouette were found by particle swarm optimization algorithm. Since the depth sensor generates point clouds, iterative nearest neighbour and its extension methods are generally used for hand estimation, which finds the best bone transformation to minimize the point-to-point correspondence distance between the model and the input point cloud.

Although model-based methods perform well in controlled environments, they still suffer from slow convergence in high-dimensional hand parameter spaces and sensitivity to initialization. In addition, all model parameters need to be estimated to find the optimal matching solution for the input image. In contrast, template-based methods can directly infer pose parameters by directly matching input image features with indexed templates. On the other hand, it does not need to calculate multiple iterative calculations, thus greatly reducing the computational consumption, and the pose parameter constraints are automatically included in the template of the dataset when the hand moves. In general, this method often needs to build a huge dataset to cover all possible hand poses, and the templates in the dataset need to contain certain features to facilitate matching, and the dataset also needs to be indexed for fast search. During the testing phase, pose estimation is achieved by finding approximate features in the dataset.

The template-based methods mainly map image features into the pose parameter space. Rosales and Sclaroff [16] defined a series of possible poses from the training data by some clusters and trained a function to realize the mapping between the descriptors of the low-level features of different clusters, such as moment features. Based on the mapping confidence, the pose estimation of the input image is obtained by fusing multiple candidate features, which often can only handle a limited number of hand poses. Thayananthan et al. [17] encoded hand image contours as score vectors by matching them with a predefined set of shape templates, which are used as input to retrieve several pose hypotheses using a multi-variate correlation vector machine, and then go through a correction stage to get the optimal solution. Guan et al. [18] used Isometric Self-Organizing Maps to learn non-linear mappings between image features and poses, which reduce dataset redundancy by grouping similar features and poses. Romero et al. [19] leveraged Locality Sensitive Hashing (LSH) to retrieve multiple candidate templates from the dataset based on HOG features of the input image, and then exploited temporal constraints to resolve ambiguity for gesture estimation. Wang et al. [20] used a two-colour acquisition system to acquire 6 degrees of freedom palm movements as well as simple gestures, extracted the silhouettes of both hands and encoded them as binary strings for fast retrieval in the dataset. Xu et al. [21] divided all parameters into many overlapping subsets, used LSH-based nearest neighbour search to obtain local estimates of each subset, and then further combined them with simulated annealing expectation-maximization algorithm to obtain overall pose parameters.

Since monocular colour images generally lack sufficient discriminative power for gestures, template-based methods typically retrieve a range of possible candidate poses. Sometimes, this kind of problem can be solved with multi-angle cameras and time constraints. Another common solution is to add a correction stage after the gesture retrieval stage.

Both model-based and template-based methods have their own advantages and disadvantages. Model-based methods generally converge slowly in high-dimensional gesture spaces and are sensitive to initialization. The template-based method requires a large number of training samples to cover the hand motion parameter space, and usually produces ambiguous prediction results. Due to the discreteness of its sample set, it can only obtain discrete prediction results. Therefore, combining the two can complement each other and fully exploit the advantages of both.

As above discussed, the correction stage following the discriminative pose retrieval stage employs a model-based approach. Conversely, pose retrieval is also applied in the initialization phase of model-based methods. Wei et al. [22] proposed a 3D model-based pose tracking framework, in which the human body size of the input image may have many kinds, and the random forest classifier provides a preliminary body parsing method for fitting the real input to the 3D model as initialization. Baak et al. [23] extracted the geodesic extremum features from the depth image and used it to construct a feature template set. During prediction, some candidate values were retrieved from the template set, and the other part was obtained by fitting the body mesh model and the depth image. The result is obtained from a comprehensive consideration of all candidate values.

Noting that hand semantic segmentation can remove unreasonable hand parameter configurations, thereby helping to reduce the search space of hand parameters, many methods utilize pre-trained classifiers to localize them to facilitate full-degree-of-freedom pose estimation. Ballan et al. [24] proposed a model-based framework to capture very small hand movements through 8 high definition cameras from multiple angles, detect fingernails at different angles using Hough forest classifier and use image contours and optical flow to fit a hand model. Sridhar et al. [25] detected fingertips through a SVM classifier and HOG features, and then inferred the hand parameters through an offline synthetic dataset to obtain several candidate values. At the same time, other candidate values are obtained by fitting the generated model, and finally the optimal solution is selected by selecting the smallest matching error from these two groups of candidate values. A similar method framework is also applied in the work of Qian et al. [7], where protruding fingertips are detected by morphological operations, and partial gestures are estimated from the possibly incomplete 3D coordinates of fingertips and used as initial values for subsequent model fitting, which can speed up the convergence process and avoid getting trapped in local optimal solutions.

2. Discriminative Approach
The discriminative method mainly learns a mapping relationship between the observed features and the predicted output, that is, the corresponding pose parameters are directly estimated from the input image. There are generally two methods: Random Forest (RF) and Neural Network (NN).

The feasibility of combining random forests and spatial voting for human pose estimation is first shown. A random forest classifier by Shotton et al. [26] was trained to classify each pixel of the depth image into a different body semantic block, and the joint point coordinates were searched using the Mean-Shift algorithm based on the parsing of the body parts. Girshick et al. [27] proposed a method to directly regress body joint points from depth images. Based on the RF model obtained by training, each pixel votes on which joint position it belongs to, and the votes of all pixels are fused, and the Mean-Shift algorithm is used to find the final prediction result. This method is computationally fast and can even infer occluded joints. However, when the input is defective, the independent voting results will tend to be multiple outcomes, and the mean-shift algorithm will also fall into the wrong results. Sun et al. [28] improved the performance of random forest models by modelling specific body parameters, such as orientation, height, etc. Then it is also used as the estimation problem of articulated objects, and the random forest algorithm starts to be applied to gesture estimation. Xu et al. [29] proposed a random forest model that directly regresses the coordinates of hand joint points from the depth map. Using a pre-trained forest model, each pixel votes on the joint angle separately, and all the voting results are fused to obtain a series of candidates, and then go through the correction stage to get the optimal solution. A similar approach was also applied to the work of Tang et al. [30], which utilized transfer learning to handle the discrepancy between synthetic and real data based on novel features. Kirac et al. [31] adopted the random forest model to predict gestures. In order to solve the ambiguous prediction, a series of candidate coordinates were first found for each joint point through model search, and then dynamic planning was used to obtain the optimal combination of the coordinates of different joint points according to the constraints of bone length, however, the bone length constraint cannot fully describe the gesture space. Therefore, this method can only be applied to a fixed hand size and cannot be applied to different users. Poudel et al. [32] used the Markov model to strengthen dynamic constraints and temporal consistency. Tang et al. [33] merged multiple layers of information and used a Latent tree model to partition the hand, and the hand hierarchy can be embedded in the training phase, and each regression tree is structured so that all joints can be estimated at once.

In general, the successful application of random forest-based methods is mainly attributed to two parts: First, random forests can run fast in both training and testing phases and are suitable for parallel computing, whilst being robust to label noise. Especially for high-dimensional input, it has good effect, so it is suitable for estimation of hand pose. Second, these methods utilize spatial voting techniques to aggregate estimated parameters and are therefore insensitive to defective inputs.

Many researchers have used random forest to regress the joint point coordinates from the depth map and achieved good results. However, this method requires pixel-level calibration of the depth map, which requires too much data. With the rise of deep learning, more and more scholars have begun to adopt the method of deep neural network. The existing methods of estimating gestures from depth maps mainly have two strategies: one is to first divide into several blocks and then build an intermediate representation model to perform joint point estimation; the other is to directly regress the joint point coordinates from the depth map.

Tompson et al. [34] first used a slower generative method to obtain label data, and then trained a convolutional neural network model. Taylor et al. [35] adopted a conditionally constrained Boltzmann machine for human pose tracking and achieved high accuracy, which employed 4 camera perspectives. Hafiz et al. [36] proposed a complex-valued neural network for gesture recognition, whose input used RGB images and depth images, and then used it to obtain hand skeleton parameters. Toshev and Szegedy [37] regressed the 2D human pose by directly optimizing the pose prediction value of the training data. Compared with the traditional method, the results showed excellent performance. However, the training time was longer, and it was not suitable for larger datasets. Tompson et al. [38] proposed a hybrid network including convolutional neural network and MRF for human pose estimation, CNN as a region detector, and then MRF as a spatial model to represent the spatial location distribution of body parts. This multi-stage idea is also applied in the work of Sinha et al. [39], Oberweger [40] and Neverova et al. 41], Sinha et al. [39] divided the prediction stage into global regression and local regression, whilst Oberweger et al. [40] split the network into an initialization stage and an optimization stage, Neverova et al. [41] used weak supervision to form two networks with two different inputs, which in turn learn to supervise each other.

Another common approach is to first generate a 2D heatmap corresponding to the joint points, and then estimate the joint point parameters from the heatmap. Tompson et al. [34] and Ge et al. [42] adopted this idea, that is, using a 2D heatmap to divide the network into several stages, and using image pyramids or multi-view images to form a multi-resolution network.

Similar to the random forest problem, the first strategy is only effective when applying synthetic data, where the relay labels can be easily and automatically obtained. For real data, accurate block division calibration is difficult to achieve. On the other hand, compared with the joint point data, the block division strategy needs to give the information of each pixel, so the information passed to the algorithm is significantly increased.

2.1.3 Summary

Hand gesture recognition as a classic human–computer interaction method has explored a variety of techniques during its development. Early methods mainly utilize the marker-related approach, such as data gloves. Leveraging the suitable marker design, accurate hand gesture recognition can be achieved, but this kind of method is clumsy and expensive. This has led to more studies using lower-cost camera sensors as acquisition devices without marker peripherals to achieve the most natural interaction. The generative methods used in the early stage are more complex, generally requiring multiple assumptions, and need to design a criterion for evaluating the matching degree of the input image and the 3D model. However, establishing this criterion is not a simple task, and it is also easily affected by initialization. The random forest method requires pixel-level calibration of the image, which is laborious. Deep learning technology has seen tremendous success in a variety of fields, and it is currently the most popular approach for hand gesture recognition due to its accuracy and robustness. Therefore, this chapter will focus on introducing and discussing the state-of-the-art deep learning-based methods for the vision-based hand gesture recognition.

2.2 Depth Sensor-Based Hand Pose Estimation

The goal of hand pose estimation is to obtain the 3d joint points information of the hand. As a result, it is widely used in VR applications to enhance immersion and interactivity due to it can synchronize the virtual state with the physical pose. Compared with colour images, depth images can obtain more three-dimensional structural information of the hand surface, which can greatly reduce the ambiguity in prediction, and can cope with the challenges brought by complex background and lighting. Therefore, the depth sensor is a more suitable acquisition device for 3d hand pose estimation.

2.2.1 Neural Network Basics

The NN is a classic multi-layer structure model. A typical NN structure consists of input layer x, output layer y, and several hidden layers h containing several neurons, as shown in Fig. 2.5. Usually, for each neuron h_j in the hidden layer, it is obtained by multiplying all neurons x_i in the previous layer by the corresponding weight w_{ij} and then adding it through a non-linear function, as shown in the following:

$$h_j = f\left(\sum_i w_{ij} x_i + b_j\right) \qquad (2.1)$$

Fig. 2.5 The classic NN with 3 layers

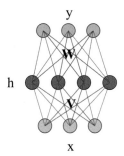

where w_{ij} is the connection weight between two adjacent layers of neurons, b_j is the bias term, and $f()$ is a non-linear function, usually called an activation function, commonly used Sigmoid, Tanh, Rectified Linear Unit (ReLU), etc.

Although the NN model has been proposed as early as the 1960s, it has not received much attention. The main reasons are as follows: (1) The relevant theoretical foundations in the early stage were incomplete, for example, the simple Exclusive OR problem can only be solved by extending the perceptron to a multi-layer structure, and the training problem can only be solved by the emergence of the back-propagation algorithm.; (2) The training data is insufficient, and the hardware is outdated. Since the neural network can easily contain a large number of weight parameters, it requires a large amount of training data and calculation resources, this was a very difficult challenge at the time; (3) Gradient dispersion, when the NN is deepened, the network weights will not be updated after a certain number of training iterations, making it impossible to converge to the local optimum, and the training is forced to be terminated in advance.

With the continuous development of hardware technology and the continuous accumulation of data, Hinton et al. [43] proposed a layer-by-layer pre-training method. Based on the Restricted Boltzmann Machine, the unsupervised learning method is used to enable each layer to reconstruct the input data of the layer, and the network is pre-trained. Finally, the back-propagation algorithm is used to optimize and fine-tune the overall network. The purpose of this layer-by-layer pre-training is to solve the problem that gradient dispersion will appear after the neural network is deepened, which makes it difficult to train, and at the same time, the network does not need a large number of training samples, because this unsupervised method can make the network weights have better initial value, so that it is easy to converge to a local optimum. Using this technique, Hinton et al. [43] stacked neural networks into multiple layers and proposed a deep belief network, which was successfully applied to face recognition and made neural networks re-focused by scholars.

The CNN is a NN model that is very suitable for computer vision tasks. It can effectively extract multi-level representations of images by using convolution kernels. CNNs have achieved great success in computer vision mainly due to two key design concepts. The first is the local receptive field. For an image, the spatial relationship of the image is roughly proportional to the distance of the pixels, that is, the closer pixels are closely related, whilst the farther pixels are less related. Therefore, the CNN makes the neurons do not need to perceive the global image through the local connection, but only needs to perceive the local field, and then integrate the local features at a higher level to obtain the global information. This idea of local connectivity is also inspired by the structure of the visual system in biology, where neurons in the visual cortex only respond to stimuli in certain regions. By further sharing the weights, the weights required by the CNN are further greatly reduced. Secondly, the pooling operation makes the network have a certain degree of translation invariance and can also make the network have a larger receptive field layer by layer. The change of the receptive field makes each layer produce different degrees of abstract representation of the input. For example, for the target detection task, the convolutional neural network focuses on the local information such as the edge of the target in the early stage and pays more attention to the whole target in the later stage.

Most of the current CNN structures used in computer vision tasks are influenced by the successful application of LeNet proposed by LeCun in 1998 to handwritten font recognition [44], which identifies four operations of typical CNN: (1) Convolutional layer; (2) Non-linear excitation; (3) Normalization layer; 4. Pooling layer. Although CNNs require very few weights compared to fully connected classical NNs, they still rely on a large amount of labelled data and computational resources.

2.2.2 CNN Model for Hand Pose Estimation

The hand pose estimation can be thought of as extracting the hand joint points from an image, and the output is the 3D coordinates of the J joint points representing the corresponding hand pose. We express the coordinates of the J joint points by the following:

$$\varphi = \phi_{j=1}^{J} \in \Lambda \qquad (2.2)$$

where Λ represents the $3 * J$-dimensional hand joint point vector space, usually $J = 14$. The positional relationship of the joints is similar to the one shown in Fig. 2.1, mainly including the wrist joint points, fingertip points, finger joint points, and palm joint points, the corresponding pose can be determined by obtaining the positions of these 14 keypoints.

1. Hand Extraction

In hand gesture recognition, the basic step is hand segmentation or hand extraction, which aims to discard the background and extract the hand part for downstream recognition and estimation tasks. A commonly used method is based on skin colour threshold. The other approach is to utilize a detection model; however, it relies on extra computational resources. Current depth sensors typically provide RGB images calibrated with depth maps to form RGB-depth (RGB-D) sensors. Therefore, the RGB image can be utilized to extract the hand area to reduce the computation. For skin colour detection, the RGB colour are generally converted to the YCrCb colour space. Because in the YCrCb colour space, the brightness and colour information are separated, the Y component represents the brightness value, and Cr and Cb represent the colour information, which can improve the robustness to changes in illumination conditions. At the same time, it has been proved by experiments that the skin colour has better aggregation in the YCrCb colour space. Through research, Hsu et al. [45] found that human skin colour is elliptically distributed on the CrCb plane, so they proposed an elliptical skin colour clustering model, as shown in the following formula:

$$\frac{(x-Cx)^2}{a^2} \cos\theta + \frac{(y-Cy)^2}{b^2} \sin\theta = 1 \tag{2.3}$$

Let the mean of the Cr and Cb components in the sample set be μ_{Cr} and μ_{Cb}, the variance is δ_{Cr}^2 and δ_{Cb}^2, and the covariance is δ_{CrCb}, then the centre coordinates:

$$(Cx, Cy) = (\mu_{Cr}, \mu_{Cb}) \tag{2.4}$$

The rotation angle:

$$\theta = \frac{1}{2} \tan^{-1}\left(\frac{2\delta_{CrCb}}{\delta_{Cr}^2 - \delta_{Cb}^2}\right) \tag{2.5}$$

The major and minor semi-axes:

$$a = \sqrt{(M+N)}, b = \sqrt{(M-N)} \tag{2.6}$$

where

$$M = 4\left(\delta_{Cr}^2 + \delta_{Cb}^2\right), N = -\frac{4\left(\delta_{Cr}^2 - \delta_{Cb}^2\right)}{\cos(2\theta)} \tag{2.7}$$

Through the experimental calculation of 500 gesture image processing, the value of each parameter is obtained, where $Cx = 110.1, Cy = 145.4, a = 24.3, b = 14.8, \theta = 42.2$.

The general process of hand extraction based on the skin colour is shown in the Fig. 2.6. The RGB-D camera can be utilized to obtain RGB colour image and the calibrated depth map at the same time. The RGB image is first converted to the YCrCb colour space, and then the values of its Cr and Cb channels are extracted, and the skin colour ellipse model is used to detect the hand area, so as to obtain the corresponding binarized image. At this time, we set the depth threshold range to [0.2, 0.5], and the unit is meter (m). The threshold range is set from two aspects: the practical interaction perspective and the effective distance from the depth sensor. By taking into account the two constraints of skin colour and depth, the hand area can finally be extracted. After obtaining the depth map of the hand area, we adjust it to a grayscale image with a size of 128 × 128, and its grayscale value represents the depth value. In order to facilitate subsequent processing, we normalize the grayscale

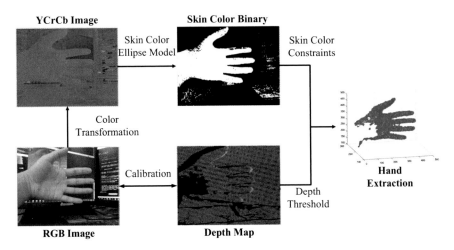

Fig. 2.6   The hand extraction pipeline based on the skin colour

value to (0, 128), that is, it is equivalent to normalizing the depth point cloud of the hand into a cube bounding box with a side length of 128. The purpose of this is to make the three-dimensional coordinates of the hand points in the same value range so that the three have influence equivalently.

2. Model Design

In the application of hand pose estimation, the input of the model is usually a single frame image, and the output is a series of coordinate values of joint points. The essence of the model is to learn a non-linear mapping from input to output. Since the input is the image, the CNN model is used as the feature extractor for two main reasons: First, compared with the fully connected NN, the weight sharing strategy adopted by the CNN greatly reduces the number of weights of the network which makes the network more efficient. It is easy to train and reduce the problem of over-fitting; the second is to have a local receptive field, because the spatial connection of local pixels is relatively close, and the correlation of pixels with farther distances is weaker. Therefore, the neuron does not need to perceive the global image, but only needs to perceive the local image, and then synthesize the local features at a higher level to obtain the global information. The existing methods for hand pose estimation based on depth map mainly have two strategies: one is to first divide into several blocks and then build an intermediate representation model to estimate the joint point. The other is to regress the joint point coordinates directly from the depth map. From the recent work progress, more researchers tend to the second strategy. The reason is that the first strategy is only effective when applying synthetic data, where the labels can be easily and automatically obtained. For real data, accurate block division calibration is difficult to achieve. On the other hand, compared with the joint point data, the block division strategy needs to give the information of each pixel. Our main idea is to think that the coordinates of the keypoints of the hand are

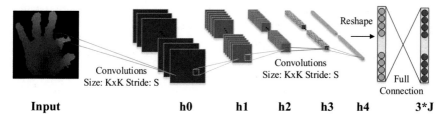

Fig. 2.7 The architecture of the proposed DC model

a sparse representation of the hand, similar to principal component analysis, which can be obtained by direct learning.

A classic CNN architecture is shown in the Fig. 2.7, called a deep convolutional neural network (DC). The input is normalized to a 128×128 depth image, and the output is a vector of length $3 * J$, which represents the three-dimensional coordinates of J joint points. The network contains 5 convolutional layers and 1 fully connected layer. The basic principle is that the size of the feature map decreases layer by layer, but the number increases layer by layer. The purpose is to ensure that the feature information does not decrease as the number of layers increases. Assume the number of the first layer feature map is c, and this parameter is a hyperparameter that will be discussed later. After that, the number of feature maps will increase by 2 times, and the size will decrease by 1/4 relationship, and the convolution kernel size is 5 $\times$ 5, the stride is 2, and the final feature map is reshaped into a one-dimensional vector, which is input to the final fully connected layer. It is worth noting that we do not use a pooling layer, but increase the stride of the convolution kernel, so that the down-sampling process of the network can also be learned.

Since the network output is the joint point coordinates, which belong to the regression task, the objective function of the network adopts the mean square error (MSE), as shown in the following formula:

$$L(y, f(x)) = \text{MSE}(y, f(x)) + \frac{\lambda}{2}||w||_2$$
$$= \frac{1}{n}\sum_{i=1}^{n}\left(y_i - y_i'\right)^2 + \frac{\lambda}{2}||w||_2 \tag{2.8}$$

where y_i' is the network output value, y_i is the corresponding expected value, that is, the label value, $\frac{\lambda}{2}||w||_2$ is the regular term, λ is the penalty coefficient, $||w||_2$ is the $L2$ norm of the model weight.

Two commonly used activation functions in traditional neural networks are Sigmoid and Tanh. The activation function is the core of the neural network, which ensures the non-linearity of the neural network. From a mathematical point of view, the non-linear sigmoid function has a large signal gain in the central area, and a small signal gain in the two side areas and has a good effect on the feature space mapping of the signal. From the perspective of neuroscience, the central area resembles the excitatory state of neurons, and the bilateral areas resemble the inhibitory state of neurons. Therefore, in terms of neural network learning, key features can be pushed to the central area, and non-key features can be pushed to both sides. Compared with the Sigmoid system, the commonly used ReLU function has three main changes: unilateral inhibition, sparse activation, and linear excitation.

In addition to sparsity, the biggest characteristic of the ReLU is the linear excitation end. Over decades of machine learning development, we have developed the notion that non-linear activation functions are more advanced than linear activation functions. Especially in the back propagation (BP) neural network that uses a large number of sigmoid functions, there is often such an illusion that non-linear functions contribute greatly to non-linear networks. This illusion is more serious in SVM, and the form of kernel function is not entirely the main contributor to SVM's ability to process non-linear data (support vector acts as a hidden layer). Then in deep networks, the degree of dependence on non-linearity can be slowed down. In addition, sparse features do not require the network to have a strong processing linear inseparability mechanism. Therefore, the deep learning model may be more appropriate to use a simple and fast piecewise linear activation function.

The biggest advantage of ReLU is that it alleviates the gradient disappearance problem when training deep networks. Anyone who understands the principle of BP knows that when the error is backpropagated from the output layer to calculate the gradient, each layer must be multiplied by the input neuron value of the current layer and the first derivative of the activation function, which is $Grad = Error \cdot f'(x) \cdot x$. There will be two problems: (1) $Sigmoid'(x) \in (0, 1)$ the derivative scaling; (2) $x \in (0, 1)$ or $x \in (-1, 1)$ the saturation scaling. In this way, the gradient decays exponentially every time it passes through a layer. Once the recursive multi-layer backpropagation is performed, the gradient will continue to decay and disappear resulting in the network learning slower. The gradient of ReLU is 1, and only one end is saturated. The gradient flows well in the backpropagation, and the training speed is greatly improved.

The ReLU enables the network to introduce sparsity, and only negative values will be sparse, that is, the introduced sparsity can be adjusted by training and changes dynamically. As long as the gradient training is performed, the network can automatically adjust the sparse ratio in the direction of reducing the error to ensure that there are a reasonable number of non-zero values in the activation chain. This approach is equivalent to pre-training of the unsupervised learning. However, the problem with ReLU is also obvious, that is, after being suppressed, it will not be able to be activated again. For example, when a very large gradient flows through a ReLU neuron and the parameters are updated, the neuron will no longer activate on any data. Leaky ReLU and Parametric ReLU are used to solve this problem [46]. Unlike the ReLU, they retain some values of the negative axis, so that the information of the negative axis will not be completely lost, that is to say, the gradient on the negative axis will no longer be 0, but a small constant. Therefore, Leaky ReLU is mainly used as the activation function in the proposed models of this book.

3. Data Augmentation

In order to avoid overfitting and improve the generalization ability of the model, it is usually necessary to input a sufficient amount of data. However, since the labelling of the hand is a laborious task, the method of data augmentation is required to expand the dataset. There are roughly two ways of data enhancement: (1) Data wrapping, which refers to performing various operational transformations on training samples in the data space, such as rotation, scaling, translation, scale transformation, etc. It often requires certain domain knowledge; (2) Synthetic over-sampling, which refers to synthesizing samples in the feature space, which does not require domain knowledge, and does not depend on specific applications. Generally, the well-designed data wrapping method is better than the synthetic resampling method, and its effect is also related to the model used. Although there is no theoretical proof for the effect of data augmentation, it is intuitively believed that adding artificial data can improve the performance of the model. It has been shown by practice, and the work of Stamatescu et al. [47] has basically verified the above hypothesis.

In the hand pose estimation, the input of the network is composed of a grayscale image converted from a depth map, and the grayscale value determines the value of the depth direction of the joint point. Therefore, this task mainly adopts three methods for data augmentation: (1) 3D random cropping. Different from general 2D pruning, we utilize 3D random pruning by moving the 3D coordinates of the bounding box within a certain range, as shown in the left of Fig. 2.8; (2) Noise disturbance. For current depth sensors, the collected data inevitably has noise and missing data, so adding Gaussian noise can improve the robustness of the network, as shown in the middle of the Fig. 2.8; (3) Hole perturbation, as mentioned above, in order to improve the robustness of the network to missing data, holes can be randomly added to the dataset, as shown in the right of Fig. 2.8.

4. Available Dataset

To facilitate the method verification analysis, this chapter introduces the commonly used hand pose dataset of New York University (NYU): NYU hand pose dataset [34]. The dataset includes 72,000 training data and 8000 test data, all of which are RGB-D data collected by Primesense Carmine which is based on structured light, and the collected depth map has data missing due to edge occlusion noise. In this experiment, we only use depth map data. The dataset has accurate annotations, and different poses have high variability. The training dataset includes data collected from

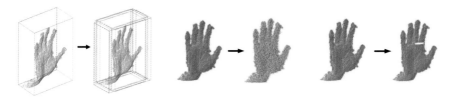

Fig. 2.8 The three kinds of data augmentation approaches

one user, whilst the test dataset includes data collected from two different users. The annotation includes $J = 36$ joint points, but we only use 14 nodes.

Compared with other datasets, the NYU has the following advantages: (1) The difference between different poses is more obvious and the diversity of the dataset is better; (2) There are more annotation points, although only 14 joint points are used in this experiment, the purpose is to facilitate subsequent comparison with other methods, and more annotation points can facilitate more accurate estimation in the future; (3) When collecting data, the distance between people and the camera is relatively moderate, and there is a larger space for activities in the image, which is more in line with our original intention of using it in virtual reality scenes.

The performance of deep neural networks depends on the choice of hyperparameters. For the sake of comparison, we choose to use the same hyperparameters for each method and make them the best configuration parameters. However, the network structure has a greater impact on the performance of the neural network, so we pay more attention to the network structure. By training different structures, the objective function is to minimize the Euclidean distance between the predicted value and the label value, and at the same time the data augmentation, weight regularization, and dropout are utilized to prevent the occurrence of overfitting. The regularization is mainly applied to the convolutional layer, and the penalty coefficient is 0.01. The training set is expanded by 10 times leveraging the data augmentation. The training optimization algorithm adopts RMSprop. The learning rate is 0.0002, the mini-batch size is 128, total of 5 epochs are per-formed, and each epoch is iterated 12,000 times.

In order to have an intuitive quantitative evaluation of the prediction results, we use two evaluation criteria: (1) Evaluation metric 1#: Calculate the mean absolute error between the predicted value and the ground truth of all samples in the test set, that is, mean absolute error (MAE), which can make a macro judgement on the predicted result; set the predicted value of a certain sample $Y' = \{y_1', y_2', \ldots, y_{3*J}'\}$, the corresponding ground truth is $Y = \{y_1, y_2, \ldots, y_{3*J}\}$, then the mean absolute error of the single sample is:

$$\text{MAE} = \frac{1}{3*J} \sum_{t=1}^{3*J} |y_t - y_t'|) \tag{2.9}$$

The corresponding mean absolute error of a certain joint point is:

$$\text{MAE}_j = \frac{1}{3} \sum_{t=1}^{3} |y_t - y_t'|) \tag{2.10}$$

(2) Evaluation metric 2#: Specify a maximum threshold as θ. When the distance between each value in the predicted value and the corresponding ground truth is less than the threshold, the predicted value is considered be correct. Finally, the proportion of correct samples in a batch of test samples is calculated, which is the accuracy rate which is as follows:

$$\text{Accuracy} = \frac{1}{N}\sum_{i=1}^{N} 1\{|Y_i - Y_i'|\}, \theta \tag{2.11}$$

where the function $1\{Y, \theta\}$ indicates that when each value in the vector Y is less than the constant θ, it returns 1, otherwise it returns 0, and $|Y_i - Y_i'|$ represents the absolute value of the different vector between the predicted vector and the ground truth vector. Compared with the first evaluation metric, this metric is more stringent. It pays more attention to local bad values and ensures that each point is correctly predicted. Otherwise, a misplaced point will cause the sample to be wrong, no matter how many other values are predicted correctly.

In the design of the network model, we mentioned that the feature map number parameter c is a hyperparameter. Therefore, we first did a set of control experiments in order to determine a better value, that is, set c equal to 16, 32, 64, 128, 256. The experimental results are shown in Fig. 2.9. It can be seen that when c increases, the error decreases accordingly. The reason is that the number of feature maps increases can enhance learning ability of the model, and the fitting performance is better. However, when it is further increased, such as when it increases to 256, the error becomes larger, and overfitting occurs at this time. Therefore, we choose $c = 128$. It is worth noting that because our sampling is relatively sparse, we only sample 5 parameters according to the exponential multiplication rule of two, so $c = 128$ is not the global optimal value, but we only use it as a basic benchmark, this book pays more attention to the impact of the network structure on the results, because the structural change has a greater impact than the selection of hyperparameters, and the selection of c is also related to the training sample size. Therefore, it is not meaningful to pursue its global optimal value too much.

In order to illustrate the advantages of the proposed DC, we compared with some classical regression methods, including multi-layer perceptron (MLP), decision tree (DT), nearest neighbour (NNb) and so on.

The MLP is a classic artificial neural network model, which belongs to shallow network to obtain a mapping equation from input to output $f(\cdot) : R^m \rightarrow R^0$, where m is the size of the input dimension and 0 is the size of the output dimension. For a set

Fig. 2.9 The evaluation results of the proposed model with different c

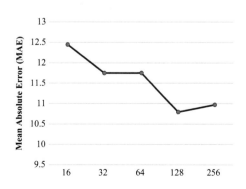

of feature sets $X = x_1, x_2, \ldots, x_m$ and the corresponding labels y, it can learn a non-linear approximation function for classification or regression problems. Different from logistic regression, the MLP directly contains one or more hidden layers in the input layer and output layer, so that it can learn almost any non-linear model, but because its layers are directly connected in the form of full connection, so the network weight will increase exponentially with the increase of the number of layers, so that the network cannot be deepened, and generally three layers are used. In this group of experiments, the number of neurons in the hidden layer is 512.

The DT is a classic non-parameter supervised learning method, its purpose is to learn some simple decision rules from the feature set, these rules will constitute a predictable model. The deeper the tree, the more complex the decision rule and the stronger the corresponding fitting ability. Compared with black-box models such as artificial neural networks, DTs are white-box models, which are easy to understand and explain, and can be visualized. However, when processing more samples, it is easy to learn an overly complex tree model, resulting in overfitting. Therefore, it is generally necessary to avoid this situation by pruning and other operations. At the same time, the DT is more sensitive to training data, and a completely different tree model may be obtained with small data fluctuations. In this experiment, the minimum number of samples for internal node division is (2), and the minimum number of samples for leaf nodes is (1) The selection strategy for feature division points is to find the optimal division point. All feature numbers are considered when dividing, and the subtree depth is not limited when the subtree is established.

The NNb is a non-generalized machine learning method, because it simply "remembers" all training samples. It makes predictions by finding several samples that are closest to the predicted samples from the training samples. The number of samples can be a user-defined constant, or it can be based on local density points. As a parameter-free method, it has been successfully applied to many classification problems. When it is used for regression problems, it calculates the average of the NNb labels as the prediction output, so the training set labels are required to be as continuous as possible. In this experiment, the NNb method based on KNN is used, the number of NNb is 5, the search algorithm is KD-Tree, the number of leaf node samples is 30, and the distance measure uses $L2$ norm.

By comparing these four methods, the average error is shown in Fig. 2.10. Although the parameters of each method are not optimal, they can basically reflect their respective abilities. It can be seen that the DC is obviously better. Compared with the other three classical methods, MLP performs the worst. For these four methods, we can simply divide: the DC is a more complex deep model; the DT and NNb are both based on building complex models for prediction, which can be considered as simple deep models, and the performance of these two methods is more similar, whilst the MLP is a shallow model. As a result, we can conclude that the DC is better suited for processing the more complex non-linear problem of gesture estimation.

In order to further compare and analyse these four methods, we use the second evaluation metric 2# to evaluate the respective prediction results, as shown in Fig. 2.11. It can be found that the DC still has the best performance. Interestingly, it can be seen that the curves of DC and MLP are relatively similar, whilst the curves

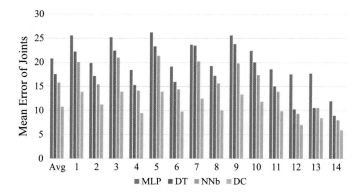

Fig. 2.10 The comparison with the classic methods

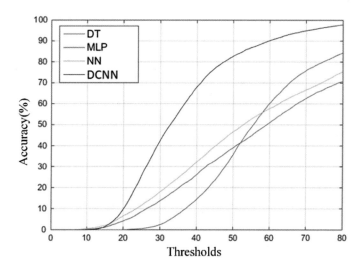

Fig. 2.11 The accuracy under different thresholds

of DT and NNb are relatively similar, because the former two belong to the neural network model, the difference lies in the deep and shallow layers, and the latter two are non-parameter models, they are both based on the approximate search of the tree model and training samples, so the performance is relatively similar. Combining the two figures, it can be concluded that the performance of the NNb is better than that of DT, but the speed of NNb is extremely slow in prediction, whilst the DT method is more practical. This also proves from the other hand that hand pose estimation mostly adopts the DT-based method before deep learning became popular. In addition, it can be seen from Fig. 2.11 that the curves of DT and NNb change more uniformly than the other two due to they use uniform approximation, so that the output errors of each node are more uniform, whilst DC and MLP belong to generalized regression models, which are greatly affected by input changes, and the prediction error variance obtained when the input has large defects. Therefore, compared to MLP, DT and NNb have lower overall average error and better performance when the threshold is not high, but MLP performs better when the threshold is high.

5. Visualization

We randomly selected various poses with different styles for evaluation, we superimposed the prediction results with the input point cloud, as shown in Fig. 2.12. When the point cloud is relatively complete, it can be well predicted. Since the NYU dataset uses the collected data from structured light sensors, this type of sensor has the problem of data missing, which will affect the accuracy of the final prediction. However, losing only a portion of the information has little effect on the prediction results, so the proposed DC model is robustness. When there is a lot of missing information, as shown in the last two rows, it will result in large errors, but it can still keep some hand structural features.

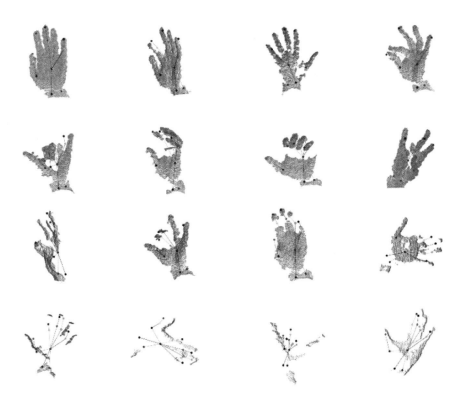

Fig. 2.12 Visualization of the predictions of the proposed model

In this section, the traditional machine learning model and the current popular multi-layer structure model are mainly introduced and discussed, and the convolutional neural network is applied to hand pose estimation, and a basic deep convolutional neural network (DC) is constructed. To improve the generalization and robustness of the model, the data augmentation approach is also utilized. Experiments show that the proposed DC is better than the traditional classical regression method, but there is still a lot of room for improvement. Compared with model parameter tuning, we prefer to optimize the model from the structural perspective, and the change of the structure has a greater impact on the model effect.

We know that for machine learning and pattern recognition, the two most important factors are: data and features. One of the reasons for the success of deep learning models represented by convolutional neural networks is the realization of autonomous learning of the multi-levels of features. Therefore, this chapter will continue to optimize the design of the network to enhance the representation capability of the model, thereby reducing the prediction error and improving the robustness.

2.2.3 Multi-scale Optimization

The neural network is a model that simulates neurons in the human brain. The connections of neurons in the human brain are sparse. Therefore, researchers believe that a reasonable connection method for large neural networks should also be sparse. Sparse structure is very suitable for neural networks, especially for large neural networks, which can reduce overfitting and reduce the amount of computation. For example, convolutional neural networks are sparse connections. The main goal of Inception Net proposed by the Google team is to find the optimal sparse structural unit [48–50]. The convolution kernel is used to connect neuron nodes with high correlation. At the same time, multiple branches with different sizes of convolution are used to increase the diversity and construct a very efficient sparse structure that conforms to the Hebbian principle. Motivated by this, we adopt a convolutional neural network with a multi-branch structure of different layers, as shown in Fig. 2.13. Since the depth map tends to have many repetitive local features (such as fingertips), the CNN is very suitable for feature extraction due to the characteristics of multi-level feature sharing, resulting in reducing the number of required weights.

Many researchers use a multi-resolution network architecture, which first builds an image pyramid, then sends feature maps of different resolutions into a variety of network branches, and finally merges the different branches together to get the output result [51]. This type of method is similar to our method, both of which utilize feature information of different resolutions. The convolutional network pays more attention to local features as the resolution is smaller in the front and focuses on the overall features as the resolution is higher in the deep layer. Combining the two can effectively improve the network performance. The difference is that our introduced method does not need to build an image pyramid in advance, which uses

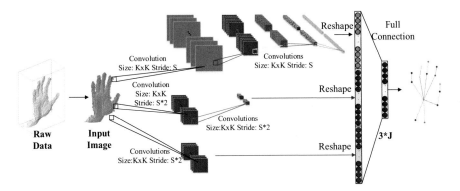

Fig. 2.13 The architecture of the multi-scale convolutional neural network

the convolution to scale the image. Therefore, the scaling process can also be learned to achieve the fusion of different levels of features.

From the perspective of gradient propagation, the multi-scale structure paper can improve the convergence speed. Below we will discuss from a formula perspective. First, we define the squared error objective function:

$$L_N = \frac{1}{2} \sum_{n=1}^{N} \sum_{k=1}^{c} \left(y_k^n - z_k^n\right)^2 \tag{2.12}$$

where N is the number of samples, c is the label dimension, y_k^n represents the k-th dimension of the label y^n of the n-th sample, and z_k^n is the k-th dimension of the prediction value of the n-th sample. The goal is to minimize L to update the weights of the network so that the network output z is closer to the ground truth y. For the convenience of illustration, we only consider the case of one sample, then the error function of the n-th sample is:

$$L_n = \frac{1}{2} \sum_{k=1}^{c} \left(y_k^n - z_k^n\right)^2 \tag{2.13}$$

Define the output of layer l as:

$$x^l = f\left(u^l\right) = f\left(W^l x^{l-1} + b^l\right) \tag{2.14}$$

where f is the activation function, x^{l-1} is the output of the $l-1$ layer, which is the input of the l layer, and W and b are the weights and biases, respectively. The above formula is also the classic forward propagation formula of the neural network. Each layer operates on the input (that is, the output of the previous layer) to obtain the output result, so that the images are passed layer by layer, and finally a predicted value is output. Backpropagation is to transmit the error information between the predicted value and the ground truth back to each layer and update them. Generally, the gradient descent algorithm and its deformation are used to update the weights and gradients. The update formula for gradient descent is as follows:

$$W^l_{new} = W^l_{old} - \eta \frac{\partial L}{\partial W^l_{old}}, b^l_{new} = b^l_{old} - \eta \frac{\partial L}{\partial b^l_{old}} \tag{2.15}$$

where the η is the learning rate of gradient descent. It can be seen that the gradient descent method mainly uses the loss function to let each layer get a gradient and then update it. To obtain the partial derivative of the loss function, the node sensitivity δ is defined as the rate of change of the loss, then:

$$\delta = \frac{\partial L}{\partial u} \tag{2.16}$$

$$\frac{\partial L}{\partial b^l} = \frac{\partial L}{\partial u^l} \frac{\partial u^l}{\partial b^l} = \delta^l \tag{2.17}$$

$$\frac{\partial L}{\partial W^l} = \frac{\partial L}{\partial u^l} \frac{\partial u^l}{\partial W^l} = \delta^l (x^{l-1})^T \tag{2.18}$$

Therefore, backpropagation is returning error information through sensitivity. The following is the core formula of backpropagation:

$$\delta^l = (W^{l+1})^T \delta^{l+1} \cdot f'(u^l) \tag{2.19}$$

The above is an overview of the classic BP algorithm. In CNN, the weight W is replaced by the convolution kernel k, and the weight update formula of CNN can be obtained. For the sake of simplicity, we still take the classic BP algorithm as an example. Assume we have only one input layer and one output layer, which is as follows:

$$z = f(u^0) = f(W^0 x + b^0) \tag{2.20}$$

$$\delta^0 = f'(u^0) \cdot (y^n - z^n) = \Delta_0; \frac{\partial L}{\partial W^0} = \delta^0 x$$
$$= \Delta_0 x^T; \frac{\partial L}{\partial b^0} = \delta^0 = \Delta_0 \tag{2.21}$$

$$z_{new} = f(W^0_{new} x + b^0_{new}) = f((W^0_{old} - \eta \Delta_0 x^T)x + (b^0_{old} - \eta \Delta_0))$$
$$= f((W^0_{old} x + b^0_{old}) - \eta \Delta_0(x^T x + 1)) \tag{2.22}$$

If we add a hidden layer between the input layer and the output layer, which is as follows:

$$z = f(u^1) = f(W^1 h^0 + b^1), h^0 = f(u^0) = f(W^0 x + b^0) \tag{2.23}$$

$$\delta^1 = f'(u^1) \cdot (y^n - z^n) = \Delta_1; \delta^0 = \delta^1 \cdot f'(u^0) \tag{2.24}$$

$$\frac{\partial L}{\partial W^1} = \delta^1 (h^0)^T = \Delta_1 (h^0)^T ; \quad \frac{\partial L}{\partial W^0} = \delta^0 x^T$$
$$= (W^1)^T \Delta_1 \cdot f'(u^0) x^T \tag{2.25}$$

$$\frac{\partial L}{\partial b^1} = \delta^1 = \Delta_1 ; \quad \frac{\partial L}{\partial b^0} = \delta^0 = (W^1)^T \Delta_1 \cdot f'(u^0) \tag{2.26}$$

$$z_{new} = f(W^1_{new} h^0_{new} + b^1_{new}) = f\left(W^1_{old} - \eta \Delta_1 h^0_{old}{}^T\right) h^0_{new} + (b^1_{old} - \eta \Delta_1) \tag{2.27}$$

$$h^0_{new} = f(W^0_{new} x + b^0_{new})$$
$$= f\left(\left(W^0_{old} - \eta W^1_{old}{}^T \Delta_1 \cdot f'(u^0) x^T\right) x + \left(b^0_{old} - \eta W^1_{old}{}^T \Delta_1 \cdot f'(u^0)\right)\right) \tag{2.28}$$

For the convenience of explanation, the activation function adopts the commonly used ReLU function. Then $f'(u^0) = f'(u^1) = 1$, assuming $\Delta_1 = \Delta_0 = \Delta$.
For the first case:

$$z_{new} = f(W^0_{old} x + b^0_{old} - \eta \Delta_0 (x^T x + 1)) = z_{old} - \eta \Delta (x^T x + 1) \tag{2.29}$$

For the second case, after simplification:

$$h^0_{new} = (W^0_{old} - \eta (W^1_{old})^T \Delta x^T) x + (b^0_{old} - \eta (W^1_{old})^T \Delta)$$
$$= W^0_{old} x + b^0_{old} - \eta (W^1_{old})^T \Delta (x^T x + 1) = h^0_{old} - \Delta_h \tag{2.30}$$

$$z_{new} = (W^1_{old} - \eta \Delta (h^0_{old})^T)(h^0_{old} - \Delta_h) + (b^1_{old} - \eta \Delta)$$
$$= W^1_{old} h^0_{old} - W^1_{old} \Delta_h - \eta \Delta (h^0_{old})^T h^0_{old} + \eta \Delta (h^0_{old})^T \Delta_h + b^1_{old} - \eta \Delta$$
$$= z_{old} - \left(W^1_{old} \Delta_h + \eta \Delta (h^0_{old})^T h^0_{old} - \eta \Delta (h^0_{old})^T \Delta_h + \eta \Delta\right)$$
$$= z_{old} - [W^1_{old} \eta (W^1_{old})^T \Delta (x^T x + 1) + \eta \Delta (h^0_{old})^T h^0_{old}$$
$$- \eta \Delta (h^0_{old})^T \eta (W^1_{old})^T \Delta (x^T x + 1) + \eta \Delta]$$
$$= z_{old} - \Delta_Z \tag{2.31}$$

$$\Delta_Z = W^1_{old} \eta (W^1_{old})^T \Delta (x^T x + 1)$$
$$+ \eta \Delta (W^0_{old} x + b^0_{old})^T (W^0_{old} x + b^0_{old})$$
$$- \eta \Delta (W^0_{old} x + b^0_{old})^T \eta (W^1_{old})^T \Delta (x^T x + 1) + \eta \Delta$$
$$= \eta [W^1_{old} (W^1_{old})^T - \Delta (W^0_{old} x + b^0_{old})^T \eta (W^1_{old})^T] \Delta (x^T x + 1)$$
$$+ \eta \Delta \left((W^0_{old} x + b^0_{old})^T (W^0_{old} x + b^0_{old}) + 1\right) \tag{2.32}$$

In the early stage of training, a smaller number of layers will speed up the convergence speed. Later, as the error becomes smaller and the values between the hidden layers are similar, the convergence speed of the two models is approximately equal. The multi-scale structure can be regarded as the parallel connection of the deep network and the shallow network. The deep structure can make the network have better accuracy, and the shallow network can improve the convergence speed of the network. Therefore, the multi-scale structure can improve the accuracy whilst increasing the convergence speed.

2.2.4 Multi-frame Optimization

Activities in the real world are continuous, such as car driving, human movement, and gesture changes. Therefore, the changes of each frame in activity are highly correlated. We can predict activities by changing trends, or we can interpolate information about missing frames through key frames, so inter-frame information is very important. Hand pose estimation needs to obtain the coordinates of multiple joint points. Since the hand joints have multiple degrees of freedom, the similarity between the fingers is high, and they are more flexible and easier to block each other. In the process of gesture tracking, noise is easily generated due to the fast-moving, which greatly increases the difficulty of the task. Due to the accuracy of the depth sensor and the problems of the hand pose itself, the collected data is prone to be lost, which hinders the estimation task. To solve this problem, considering the correlation between hand movements, it is hoped to introduce inter-frame information, which can alleviate the phenomenon of high prediction error caused by missing information or noise.

There are two typical models for the extraction of spatiotemporal features, one is a three-dimensional convolutional neural network (3D-CNN); the other is a RNN and its variant. Ji et al. [52] first introduced the 3D CNN to human action recognition, which utilized the 3D CNN to extract the temporal and spatial dimension features of actions and combined prior knowledge to the network to improve the recognition ability of the network. Tran et al. [53] found that 3D CNN is more suitable for extracting spatiotemporal features than 2D convolutional networks. Molchanov et al. [54] successively designed two 3D CNNs for hand gesture recognition. First, a two-channel 3D CNN was used to extract different spatial scale features. To further exploit the temporal dimension information, another recurrent 3D CNN is designed for dynamic gesture detection and classification [55]. Amongst them, 3D convolutional neural network is used for local spatiotemporal feature extraction, RNN is used to model overall features, and finally the probability values of different categories of gestures are obtained through the softmax layer.

The local receptive field and parameter sharing characteristics of CNN make it very suitable for processing image-related tasks. The RNN takes into account the temporal information, so it is used to process sequence data, such as natural language processing (NLP). How to combine them has attracted the attention of many researchers. For the multi-label image classification problem, Donahue et al. [56]

used CNN to extract the spatial features of each frame and then input them into the LSTM network, which is different from only accepting fixed-time input. Compared with traditional models, the proposed Long-term Recurrent Convolutional Network model can take an indefinite number of inputs and learn long-term dependencies. In terms of action recognition, Ng et al. [57] added an LSTM module on the basis of the dual-stream network proposed by Simonyan et al. [58], where the dual-stream network refers to two branches with different inputs to feed both spatial and temporal information into the LSTM. Feichtenhofer et al. [59] and Ma et al. [60] improved this kind of model further, but the general idea is to perform feature extraction with a two-stream convolution network and then input the extracted feature into the LSTM module for recognition. Pei et al. [61] also utilized this idea to the detection of small bowel diseases. It can be found that the current common practice is to use CNN to extract features, and then input them to the RNN/LSTM module for classification.

Since the input is a depth image, the core of the adopted model should still be a convolutional neural network. However, considering the advantages of 3D convolution and RNN in processing sequence data, this section will propose two optimization ideas: one is to redesign it as a 3D-CNN based on the DC model, which is called 3DDC; the other is to study the combination of CNN and RNN and introduce a fusion module which is called convolutional recurrent neural network (CRNN).

1. 3D CNN

In general, the CNN refers to 2D CNN which can perform convolutional feature extraction and recognition on single-frame images, but the problem is that the temporal dimension is not taken into account. In comparison, the 3D CNN can be utilized to capture the temporal and spatial feature information of consecutive frames for tackling dynamic activity recognition, as shown in Fig. 2.14.

The standard 2D convolution kernel is a 4-D vector that is (N, H, W, C), where N refers to the number of convolution kernels, H is the height of the convolution kernel, W is the width of the convolution kernel, and C is the number of channels. The standard 3D convolution kernel is a 5-D vector that is (N, D, H, W, C), which has an additional depth dimension D. The previous DC can be upgraded to 3D-DC using 3D-CNN, as shown in Fig. 2.15. The 3D convolution layer is used to extract spatiotemporal features. The network structure design principles are as follows: (1) Avoid using large convolution kernels; (2) To reduce the amount of calculation and the number of weights and prevent overfitting, the avgpool layer is used to down-sample the feature map; (3) Using convolution stride instead of pooling makes the down-sampling process learnable; (4) Increase the number of feature map channels and reduce the size of the feature map, so that the network can learn more feature information.

For 3D convolutional layers, the calculation formula is as follows:

$$l_{ij}^{xyz} = f\left(\sum_m \sum_{p=0}^{P_i-1} \sum_{q=0}^{Q_i-1} \sum_{r=0}^{R_i-1} w_{ijm}^{pqr} l_{(i-1)m}^{(x+p)(y+q)(z+r)} + b_{ij} \right) \qquad (2.33)$$

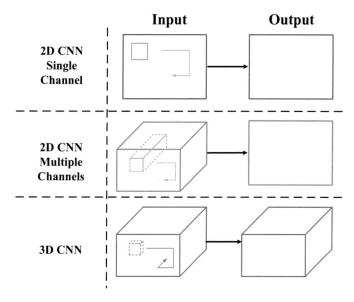

Fig. 2.14 The comparison of 2D CNN and 3D CNN

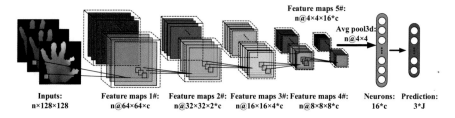

Fig. 2.15 The architecture of the 3D-DC model

where $f()$ is the activation function, l_{ij}^{xyz} is the value of the j-th feature map of the i-th layer at (x, y, z), and w_{ijm}^{pqr} is the value of the convolution kernel at (p, q, r) that performs the convolution operation with the m-th feature map of the previous layer, R_i is the time dimension of the three-dimensional convolution kernel, P_i and Q_i are the spatial dimensions of the convolution kernel, that is height and width, b_{ij} is the corresponding bias item.

2. CRNN

Compared with the 3D CNN, the RNN has more advantages and is widely used, but the typical RNN is fully connected. Therefore, an intuitive idea is to use the RNN module in the last connection layer, which has proved to be effective in many studies which utilize the convolutional layer to extract features and feed the extracted features into the RNN/LSTM module. The previous studies have demonstrated that multi-layer convolutional neural networks can extract multi-levels of features. If only the recurrent structure is added at the last layer, only the deep features can participate in the recurrent process. The question is how to involve the low-level features to improve the representation ability of the network. An intuitive idea would be to reshape the feature map to a one-dimensional vector, similar to the last connection layer; however, this will inevitably greatly increase the number of network weights, making overfitting and training difficult. Therefore, this chapter will introduce a CRNN operation module that can leverage the recurrent structure whilst keeping the convolutional operation, as shown in Fig. 2.16.

In CRNN, the different feature maps at different times of the hidden layer are:

$$h_j^t = f\left(a_h^t\right); a_h^t = \sum_{i \in M_j} x^t * v_{ij} + \sum_{i \in N_j} h^{t-1} * u_{ij} + b_j \tag{2.34}$$

where h_j^t represents the j-th feature map of the hidden layer at time t, M_j and N_j represent the selected feature maps, v_{ij} and u_{ij} are the convolution kernel used for the connection between the input i-th feature map and the output j-th feature map, b_j is the bias corresponding to the j-th feature map, and $f()$ is the activation function. The biggest difference between the CRNN module and original RNN is that the connection between layers is in the form of convolution. In Fig. 2.16, the x_i represents the input at time i, h_{i-1} represents the output of the hidden layer at time $i - 1$, h_i represents the output of the hidden layer at time i, $+$ represents the addition of the corresponding elements of the matrix, and $\oplus$ represents that each element in

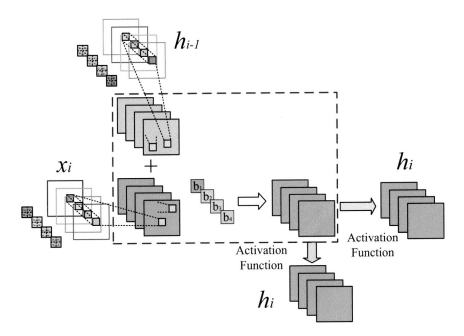

Fig. 2.16 Illustration of the CRNN module

the matrix is added with a constant, such as $A \oplus b = A + b*O$, where b is a constant and O refers to a matrix of all ones.

The above is the forward propagation process of CRNN. For backpropagation, the error is transmitted backwards from the next layer, so the different forms of the next layer determine different calculation methods. Generally, there are two forms: (1) Down-sampling layer; (2) Convolution layer. These two cases are discussed separately below.

Down-Sampling Layer
If the hidden layer is followed by a down-sampling layer, then:

$$\delta_{hj}^t = \left(\beta_j \text{up} \left(\delta_{(h+1)j}^t \right) + u_j \delta_{hj}^{t+1} \right) \Delta f'(a_h^t) \tag{2.35}$$

where h represents the hidden layer, $h + 1$ represents the next layer of the hidden layer, and t represents the t-th time. δ_{hj}^t represents the sensitivity of the j-th feature map in the hidden layer h at the t-th moment. If the $h + 1$ layer is a sampling layer, it is also equivalent to doing convolution. For example, down-sampling with scale $=$ 2 is to perform convolution operation on the image with a convolution kernel with each value of $2 * 2$ being $1/4$. Therefore, the weight w here is actually the $2 * 2$ convolution kernel, denoted as β_j. The $up()$ represents the up-sampling operation, because the sensitivity matrix of the $h + 1$ layer is $1/4$ of the size of the sensitivity matrix of the h layer (when scale $= 2$), so at this time, it is necessary to up-sample the sensitivity matrix of the $h + 1$ layer to make them the same size.

Convolutional Layer
If the hidden layer is followed by a convolutional layer, there are:

$$\delta_{hj}^t = \left(w_j \delta_{(h+1)j}^t + u_j \delta_{hj}^{t+1} \right) \Delta f'(a_h^t) \tag{2.36}$$

The gradients of the loss function to the weights and biases of the h layer are respectively:

$$\Delta b_j = \sum_t \sum_{u,v} \left(\delta_{hj}^t \right)_{u,v} \tag{2.37}$$

$$\Delta v_{ij} = \sum_t \sum_{u,v} \left(\delta_{hj}^t \right)_{u,v} \left(p_i^t \right)_{uv} \tag{2.38}$$

$$\Delta u_{ij} = \sum_t \sum_{u,v} \left(\delta_{hj}^t \right)_{u,v} \left(q_i^t \right)_{uv} \tag{2.39}$$

where (u, v) represents the element position in the sensitivity matrix, $\left(p_i^t \right)_{uv}$ is the each patch of the convolution of the x^t and v_{ij}, (u, v) is the centre of patch. The value of the (u, v) position in the output feature map is the value obtained by convoluting

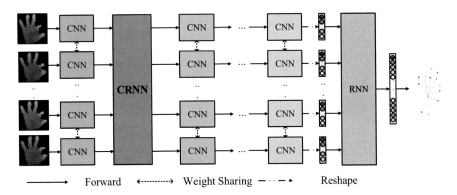

Forward   ⟵·········⟶   Weight Sharing   — ·· — ▸   Reshape

Fig. 2.17 The general framework of convolutional recurrent neural network

convolution kernel v_{ij} and the patch in the (u, v) position of the feature graph. Similarly, $\left(q_i^t\right)_{uv}$ is each patch of the convolution of the h^{t-1} and u_{ij}.

The introduced CRNN module can be added to arbitrary CNN frameworks at different positions. Therefore, the general framework of convolutional recurrent neural network is as follows in Fig. 2.17

In the figure, the CNN represents the convolutional module, the parameters are shared between the convolutional layers, and the CRNN module is located between the convolutional layers. Before the final output, the feature map is stretched to a one-dimensional vector, and then input to the final RNN module. The final output is the predicted value corresponding to the last frame of image.

3. Conclusion

The optimization direction in this section is to use the correlation information between adjacent frames. Therefore, the input of the model is transformed from general single frame information to continuous frames. Considering the advantages of RNN for processing sequence data and the advantages of CNN for processing image data, this section introduces two typical approaches: (1) Upgrade the CNN to 3D CNN, so that the model has the ability to deal with spatiotemporal features, which is characterized by relying on the model to learn temporal information which is not explicitly given. (2) Combining CNN and RNN in two ways. The RNN explicitly provides the sequential information, so it is a widely used module to tackle the sequential data. Therefore, a general framework that combines the CNN and RNN is introduced, which can be adjusted according to specific tasks and scenarios.

2.3   Efficient Dynamic Hand Gesture Recognition

Dynamic gesture recognition, as an important approach to human–computer interaction, has been studied by researchers for decades. It has been applied in many scenarios due to its natural, non-intrusive, and convenient manner, such as the AR glasses, the intelligent cockpit, the smartphone, etc. However, there are still numerous challenges due to the following factors: First, there is the flexibility and diversity of hand gesture, which means that even if the same person is performing the same action at different times, it will result in different states. In addition, various skin colours, illuminations, and other factors cause significant differences in the captured images for vision-based dynamic gesture. The second is the change in activity speed. The third is the identification of negative cases, at the beginning and end of the activity or in different stages of activity translation, the action will confuse the recognition model to have a correct classification. Lastly, the applications usually require real-time recognition to meet the expected time of the feedback (Fig. 2.18).

In dynamic gesture recognition, Hidden Markov [62, 63], SVM [64, 65], and CRF [66] have been widely used. Many hand-crafted features are developed to improve the accuracy of recognition. In recent years, the depth sensor has been combined with the RGB sensor to improve input data and recognition robustness. Deep neural networks have recently been successfully applied to a variety of recognition tasks. It attracts numerous attention due to its strong representation ability. Furthermore, the CNN can avoid the complex pre-processing to form an end-to-end learning pattern, it is widely used in image-related tasks. Many researchers have begun to introduce deep neural networks to gesture recognition with promising results as the above section mentioned. When the input to dynamic gesture recognition is the sequential images, there are currently two main methods: one that combines CNN and RNN / LSTM and the other that uses 3D CNN, which as the above mentioned. In the former method, the RNN / LSTM is fully connected, resulting in more network parameters and an increase in computation. In addition, the commonly used architecture of the

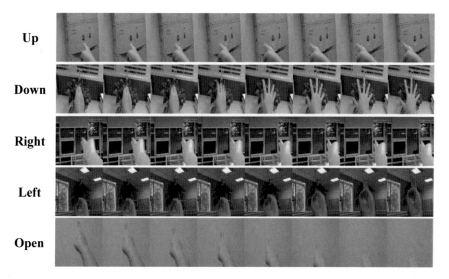

Fig. 2.18 The illustration of the dynamic hand gesture recognition

action recognition is the multi-stream structure. Diba et al. utilized a dual-stream CNN structure with optical flow and RGB images as inputs to train the network to learn video motion features, which were then classified using SVM [67]. Ng [57], Simonyan [58], Feichtenhofer [59], and Ma [68] all adopted dual-stream structures and utilized two different input branches, RGB image and optical flow. Based on the original RGB image, the optical flow can provide certain prior knowledge to the network, which causes the network to focus on moving objects and improves the network recognition performance. This concept is also adopted by this section to enhance the model performance.

Compared with the hand pose estimation, dynamic hand gesture recognition is more preferred employed in the embedding computation platform, which more emphasizes the efficiency of the computational resources. The existing studies for network compression and acceleration methods are primarily based on 2D CNN, and they can be roughly divided into two categories based on the perspective of the compression manner: network weight and network structure. In terms of computing speed, they can also be divided into two categories: only compress size and compress size whilst increasing speed. In terms of network weight, the Deep Compression model [69] and XNorNet [70] are typical work. The former reduces the weight through pruning, quantization, and Huffman coding, but it does not consider calculation speed. The latter compresses the weight through binarization, increasing calculation speed, but reducing network precision. Hinton et al. proposed a distilling algorithm similar to network transfer [71], in which a small network is taught by a large network with good performance until the small network has the same performance as the large, achieving the goal of network compression whilst leaving out network acceleration. SqueezeNet [73] was proposed to optimize the network from the structural perspective. The number of network weights was reduced by optimizing the network structure without taking the amount of computation into account, resulting in three network structure design strategies: (1) Replacing the 3×3 convolution kernel with a 1×1 convolution kernel; (2) Reducing the number of input channels; and (3) Placing the down sampling process as close to the end of the network as possible. These three strategies can provide us with some inspirations for designing the structure of the network. Google's proposed MobileNet network architecture was designed for mobile deployment [72]. Due to computing resources are limited on mobile devices, Google borrowed ideas from factorized convolution and divided the standard convolution operation into two parts: depth-wise convolution and point-wise convolution. It has the potential to increase network efficiency by 89%. In this section, we will more focus on the efficient dynamic hand gesture recognition model and introduce a novel 3d separable CNN model to reduce the model size.

2.3.1 Pre-processing

The input of the vision-based dynamic hand gesture is basically a series of n-frame images, assuming with $n = 8$ in this book. Many researchers leverage the traditional

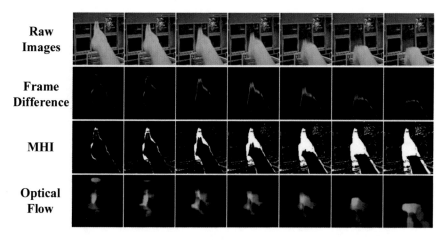

Fig. 2.19 Three typical motion detection algorithms

moving object detection algorithms to pre-process the raw images, which can introduce the prior knowledge to improve the performance of the recognition method.
The commonly utilized algorithms primarily include: (1) optical flow; (2) motion
history image (MHI); and (3) frame difference, as shown in Fig. 2.19. The optical
flow method and the frame difference method can effectively filter out useless background noise and highlight the movement of objects. The MHI method preserves
some of the background, which accumulates the noise, resulting in more background
in later MHI images. When comparing the optical flow and the frame difference, the
latter can help extract more key contour information, which aids in the downstream
recognition process. The optical flow is sluggish. Using the sample in Fig. 2.19 as an
example, the optical flow method takes 0.06 s to calculate, whereas the frame difference method takes only 0.004 s. However, the optical flow can reflect the motion
direction information, which might be beneficial to recognize some specific activities. Therefore, the researcher can choose the appropriate algorithm according to the
specific application and scenario.

2.3.2 3D CNN-Based Network Structure

Figure 2.20 depicts a typical 3D CNN model for dynamic hand gesture recognition. Its
architecture consists of a pre-processing layer for filtering background information,
a deep 3D-CNN for extracting temporal-spatial features, and a SoftMax layer for
predicting the likelihood of an object being classified into different classes. The
network's structure includes the following features: (1) The convolution kernel is 3
$\times$ 3 $\times$ 3 in size to reduce the number of weights; (2) The down sampling of temporal
dimension occurred closest to the end so that the most convolution layers can have
the most activation images; (3) The network can learn the down sampling process

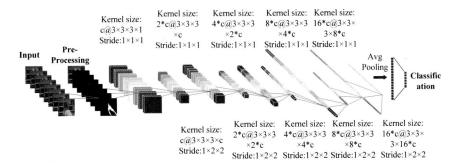

Fig. 2.20 A typical 3D CNN architecture for the dynamic hand gesture recognition

by increasing the stride rather than pooling; 4. The network would have a larger feature image by increasing the number of channels and then decreasing the size of the feature image.

We will now go over the network's operation in detail. A video clip is defined as $C \in V^{w \times h \times c \times m}$;, where m $\geq$ 1 is the time node, $w \times h$ is the image size, and C is the number of channels. The frame difference layer produces $L_0 \in (C_0, D_0, .., D_{m-2})$, where $D_i = \text{Diff}(C_{i,} C_{i+1})$ and Diff() represents the frame difference function. The $m - 1$ frame difference image is obtained by frame difference from the initial m frame images, and the first frame of the initial clip is merged with the $m - 1$ frames into the input, so the input is still m frames. Then, a variety of 3D CNN layer is utilized with different channels and strides, which formula is described in the above section. The 3D AvgPool layer is similar to the 3D CNN layer in most ways, except that the value of w is fixed and there is no bias. Finally, the feature image is reshaped into a one-dimensional vector, and the classification result is obtained via the fully connected layer.

2.3.3   Architecture Optimization

The computational cost of the 3D convolution process is:

$$D_k \cdot D_K \cdot D_K \cdot M \cdot N \cdot D_F \cdot D_F \cdot D_f \tag{2.40}$$

where M is the number of input channels, N is the number of output channels, $D_K \cdot D_K$ is the kernel size, $D_F \cdot D_F$ is the feature map size, D_k is the number of convolution kernels in the time dimension, and D_f is the number of frames. The number of parameters required for two-dimensional convolution is $D_K \cdot D_K \cdot M \cdot N$, if the total number of feature maps of two adjacent layers is fixed, and the size of the convolution kernel is fixed, that is, M, N, and $D_K \cdot D_K$ are fixed. When the convolution layer becomes a 3D convolutional layer, that is, the input and output layers are divided into several equal bins, the input layer becomes $c \cdot m = M$, and the output layer becomes $D_f \cdot n = N$, then the number of parameters required for the three-dimensional convolution is $D_k \cdot D_K \cdot D_K \cdot m \cdot n$, where $D_k \leq c$, it can be seen that the number of parameters has become to:

$$\frac{D_k \cdot D_K \cdot D_K \cdot m \cdot n}{D_K \cdot D_K \cdot M \cdot N} = \frac{D_k}{c \cdot D_f} \leq 1 \tag{2.41}$$

And the computational cost become to:

$$\frac{D_k \cdot D_K \cdot D_K \cdot m \cdot n \cdot D_F \cdot D_F \cdot D_f}{D_K \cdot D_K \cdot M \cdot N \cdot D_F \cdot D_F} = \frac{D_k}{c} \leq 1 \tag{2.42}$$

Therefore, from the perspective of efficiency, 3DCNN is more suitable for tackling the dynamic gesture recognition task. If we want to further compress the network structure, the simplest way is to reduce the values of the eight parameters in Eq. 2.40. We can begin by using a relatively small convolution kernel, that is, a relatively small value $D_k \cdot D_K \cdot D_K$. In this section, the convolution kernel is $3 \times 3 \times 3$ in size to ensure that the spatial–temporal feature can be extracted. Of course, we can continue to reduce the number and size of feature images by using small values of M, N, and $D_F \cdot D_F \cdot D_f$, but this method is not used to ensure feature diversity.

Howard et al. [72] reduce the computational cost of standard 2D convolution by decomposing it into depth-wise and point-wise processes. We extend this concept to 3D convolution, decomposing the standard 3D convolution process into two processes: 3D depth-wise and 3D point-wise. The convolution kernels calculated the input sequence from each channel separately in the 3D depth-wise phase, as shown in Fig. 2.21, and the convolution result was not combined. The results of the adjacent frames are later concatenated. In the point-wise phase, a convolution kernel of size $1 \times 1 \times 1$ is used for 3D convolution.

Thus, the calculation process of the 3D separable convolution becomes:

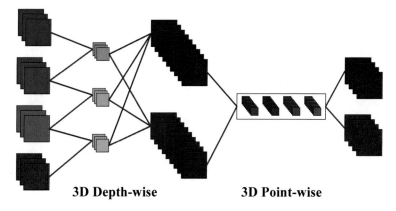

3D Depth-wise   **3D Point-wise**

Fig. 2.21 Illustration of the 3d separable convolution

$$d_{ij}^{xyz} = f\left(\sum_{p=0}^{P_{i-1}} \sum_{q=0}^{Q_{i-1}} w_{ih}^{pqk} l_{(i-1)h}^{(x+p)(y+q)(z+k)} + b_{ij}\right) \qquad (2.43)$$

$$k = \text{ceil}\left(\frac{j}{m}\right), h = j - k * m - 1 \qquad (2.44)$$

$$l_{ij}^{xyz} = f\left(\sum_m w_{ijm} d_{im}^{xyz} + b_{ij}\right) \qquad (2.45)$$

As a result, the computational cost after such decomposition is:

$$D_k \cdot D_K \cdot D_K \cdot M \cdot D_F \cdot D_F \cdot D_f + D_k \cdot M \cdot N \cdot D_F \cdot D_F \cdot D_f \qquad (2.46)$$

When compared to a standard 3D CNN, the computational cost is:

$$\frac{D_k \cdot D_K \cdot D_K \cdot M \cdot D_F \cdot D_F \cdot D_f + D_k \cdot M \cdot N \cdot D_F \cdot D_F \cdot D_f}{D_k \cdot D_K \cdot D_K \cdot M \cdot N \cdot D_F \cdot D_F \cdot D_f}$$
$$= \frac{1}{N} + \frac{1}{D_K \cdot D_K} \qquad (2.47)$$

The $3 \times 3 \times 3$ convolution kernel is used in this section, $N \geq 32$, and the amount of calculation is reduced by about 8 to 9 times. Whilst the number of parameters is being reduced:

$$\frac{D_k \cdot D_K \cdot D_K \cdot M + M \cdot N}{D_k \cdot D_K \cdot D_K \cdot M \cdot N} = \frac{1}{N} + \frac{1}{D_k \cdot D_K \cdot D_K} \qquad (2.48)$$

Its parameter count decreased by about 10–20 times. The decomposition operation can greatly reduce the number of model parameters and the amount of calculation whilst also doubling the number of layers and enhancing network non-linearity, whilst deep networks typically outperform shallow networks.

To evaluate the introduced model, we collected a dynamic gesture dataset, which includes five kinds of dynamic hand gestures: up, down, right, left, open, as shown in Fig. 2.18. The data was captured by an egocentric RGB camera from 10 people. To improve the model's prediction accuracy in practice, the dataset included images with both simple and complex backgrounds. Finally, 100K training samples and 10K test samples were created.

Our goal is to create a network that is efficient in three ways: accuracy, model size, and computational cost. The evaluation criteria are as follows: confusion matrix, average accuracy, precision, recall, and $F1$ score. The confusion matrix can be used to calculate the accuracy of predicting hand gestures from each category. The average accuracy provides an overall understanding of the network's performance. However, the average accuracy is not very informative because the numbers of positive and negative samples are not balanced. Therefore, we can use the last three criteria which are typically used for dichotomies, where the five gestures are considered as positive

Table 2.1 The comparison based on the AMI hand gesture dataset

Model	Accuracy	Precision	Recall	$F1$	Model size (MB)	Billion mult-adds
Modified inception V3	0.9122	0.6260	0.9112	0.7421	96.9	4.2
3D CNN	0.9744	0.8584	0.9769	0.9138	53.9	9.8
3D separable CNN	0.9631	0.8128	0.9539	0.8777	6.17	1.3

samples. The model's performance can be fully tested using these five metrics, and the influence of sample imbalance can be alleviated.

This section utilizes the classic Inception V3 network [49] as the benchmark method to fairly evaluate the 3D CNN models. A few modifications are implemented to enable it to be suitable for the task, and primarily include: (1) The convolutional padding type is changed from "VALID" to "SAME"; (2) The last pooling layer of the base module is abandoned; (3) The kernel size of the third layer in the aux logits branch is increased from 5×5 to 6×6.

The modified Inception V3, 3D CNN, and the 3D separable CNN are trained with the optimizer Adam using the learning rate of 0.0001. The batch size is 16, and total of 5 epochs are implemented. The experimental results can be found in Table 2.1. The comparison shows that the 3D CNN can achieve better performance on handling the sequential data and has a smaller model size, however, the computational cost is increased. The 3D separable CNN can significantly reduce model size and computational cost whilst maintaining recognition performance. It demonstrates the capability of the introduced 3D separable convolution.

To further evaluate the 3D separable CNN, the confusion matrixes of them are calculated as shown in Fig. 2.22, which can evaluate the recognition performance of the model on the different classes to avoid the effect of the imbalance dataset. The results show that the 3D separable CNN only slightly decreases the recognition accuracy. When weighed against the benefit of low computational cost, the slight decrease is manageable. The readers can choose the appropriate configuration according to the specific applications.

2.4 Summary

This chapter briefly introduces the hand activity recognition-related topics, including hand pose estimation, the static and dynamic hand gesture recognition. The research background is reviewed, and deep learning-based methods are the mainstream solution capable of achieving cutting-edge performance.

The hand pose estimation is a hot research topic due to its complexity and other challenges, which can provide an immersion interaction manner and is the essential enabling technology of the VR-related applications. This chapter presents the

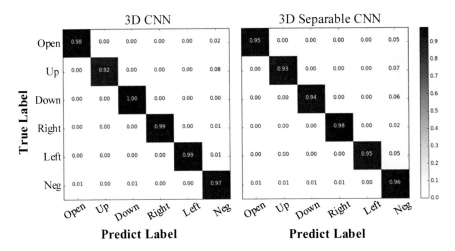

Fig. 2.22 The confusion matrixes of the standard 3D CNN and separable 3D CNN

commonly used depth sensor-based approaches, as well as several typical deep learning-based models. Recently, many researchers have begun to introduce graph neural networks to solve it, which is also a potentially promising approach. In addition, the currently most challenging problem of hand pose estimation is the situation of the hand–object interaction. At this time, most of the hands are occluded, which greatly increase the difficulty of estimation. However, this is also a very valuable question that will greatly determine the scope of application scenarios, and it is worth the related researchers pay more attention to it.

The dynamic hand gesture recognition has been deployed in many embedding application scenarios. This chapter provides a reasonable solution to improve its efficiency of the computation. Leveraging the development of the deep learning technology and the intelligent hardware, it should be further investigated to reduce the computational cost to meet the practical needs. Usually, the related applications can provide several initial gestures, but the customization approach should be further explored to achieve the personality solution.

References

1. Chua C-S, Guan H, Ho Y-K (2002) Model-based 3d hand posture estimation from a single 2d image. Image Vis Comput 20(3):191–202
2. Theobalt C, Albrecht I, Haber J, Magnor M, Seidel H-P (2004) Pitching a baseball: tracking high-speed motion with multi-exposure images. In: ACM SIGGRAPH 2004 papers, pp 540–547
3. Wang RY, Popović J (2009) Real-time hand-tracking with a color glove. ACM Trans Graph (TOG) **28**(3):1–8

4. Zhao W, Chai J, Xu Y-Q (2012) Combining marker-based mocap and rgb-d camera for acquiring high-fidelity hand motion data. In: Proceedings of the ACM SIGGRAPH/Eurographics symposium on computer animation pp 33–42
5. Ballan L, Taneja A, Gall J, Gool LV, Pollefeys M (2012) Motion capture of hands in action using discriminative salient points. In: European conference on computer vision. Springer pp 640–653
6. Oikonomidis I, Kyriazis N, Argyros AA (2011) Full dof tracking of a hand interacting with an object by modeling occlusions and physical constraints. In: 2011 International conference on computer vision. IEEE, pp 2088–2095
7. Qian C, Sun X, Wei Y, Tang X, Sun J (2014) Realtime and robust hand tracking from depth. In: Proceedings of the IEEE conference on computer vision and pattern recognition, pp 1106–1113
8. Srinath S (2016) Tracking hands in action for gesture-based computer input. Ph.D. thesis
9. Wu Y, Huang TS (1999) Capturing articulated human hand motion: a divide-and-conquer approach. In: Proceedings of the seventh IEEE international conference on computer vision, vol 1. IEEE, pp 606–611
10. Stenger, B, Mendonça PR., Cipolla R (2001) Model-based 3d tracking of an articulated hand. In: Proceedings of the 2001 IEEE computer society conference on computer vision and pattern recognition. CVPR 2001, vol 2
11. Lin JY, Wu Y, Huang TS (2004) 3d model-based hand tracking using stochastic direct search method. In: Sixth IEEE international conference on automatic face and gesture recognition, 2004. Proceedings. IEEE, pp 693–698
12. Felzenszwalb PF, Huttenlocher DP (2005) Pictorial structures for object recognition. Int J Comput Vision 61(1):55–79
13. Ueda E, Matsumoto Y, Imai M, Ogasawara T (2001) Hand pose estimation using multi-viewpoint silhouette images. In: Proceedings 2001 IEEE/RSJ international conference on intelligent robots and systems. Expanding the societal role of robotics in the next millennium (Cat. No.01CH37180), vol 4. IEEE, pp 1989–1996
14. de La Gorce M, Fleet DJ, Paragios N (2011) Model-based 3d hand pose estimation from monocular video. IEEE Trans Pattern Anal Mach Intell 33(9):1793–1805
15. Oikonomidis I, Kyriazis N, Argyros AA (2011) Efficient model-based 3d tracking of hand articulations using kinect. In: BmVC, vol 1, p 3
16. Rosales R, Sclaroff S (2000) Inferring body pose without tracking body parts. In: Proceedings IEEE conference on computer vision and pattern recognition. CVPR 2000 (Cat. No. PR00662), vol 2. IEEE, pp 721–727
17. Thayananthan A, Navaratnam R, Stenger B, Torr PH, Cipolla R (2008) Pose estimation and tracking using multivariate regression. Pattern Recogn Lett 29(9):1302–1310
18. Guan H, Feris RS, Turk M (2006) The isometric self-organizing map for 3d hand pose estimation. In: 7th International conference on automatic face and gesture recognition (FGR06). IEEE, pp 263–268
19. Romero J, Kjellström H, Kragic D (2009) Monocular real-time 3d articulated hand pose estimation. In: 2009 9th IEEE-RAS international conference on humanoid robots. IEEE, pp 87–92
20. Wang R, Paris S, Popović J (2011) 6d hands: markerless hand-tracking for computer aided design. In: Proceedings of the 24th annual ACM symposium on user interface software and technology, pp 549–558
21. Xu J, Wu Y, Katsaggelos A (2010) Part-based initialization for hand tracking. In: 2010 IEEE international conference on image processing. IEEE, pp 3257–3260
22. Wei X, Zhang P, Chai J (2012) Accurate realtime full-body motion capture using a single depth camera. ACM Trans Graph (TOG) 31(6):1–12
23. Baak A, Müller M, Bharaj G, Seidel H-P, Theobalt C (2013) A data-driven approach for real-time full body pose reconstruction from a depth camera. In: Consumer depth cameras for computer vision. Springer, pp 71–98
24. Ballan L, Taneja A, Gall J, Gool LV, Pollefeys M (2012) Motion capture of hands in action using discriminative salient points. In: European conference on computer vision. Springer, pp 640–653

25. Sridhar S, Oulasvirta A, Theobalt C (2013) Interactive markerless articulated hand motion tracking using rgb and depth data. In: Proceedings of the IEEE international conference on computer vision, pp 2456–2463
26. Shotton J, Fitzgibbon A, Cook M, Sharp T, Finocchio M, Moore R, Kipman A, Blake A (2011) Real-time human pose recognition in parts from single depth images. In: CVPR 2011. IEEE, pp 1297–1304
27. Girshick R, Shotton J, Kohli P, Criminisi A, Fitzgibbon A (2011) Efficient regression of general-activity human poses from depth images. In: 2011 International conference on computer vision. IEEE, pp 415–422
28. Sun M, Kohli P, Shotton J (2012) Conditional regression forests for human pose estimation. In: 2012 IEEE conference on computer vision and pattern recognition. IEEE, pp 3394–3401
29. Xu C, Cheng L (2013) Efficient hand pose estimation from a single depth image. In: Proceedings of the IEEE international conference on computer vision, pp 3456–3462
30. Tang D, Yu T-H, Kim T-K (2013) Real-time articulated hand pose estimation using semi-supervised transductive regression forests. In: Proceedings of the IEEE international conference on computer vision, pp 3224–3231
31. Kirac F, Kara YE, Akarun L (2014) Hierarchically constrained 3d hand pose estimation using regression forests from single frame depth data. Pattern Recogn Lett 50:91–100
32. Poudel RP, Fonseca JA, Zhang JJ., Nait-Charif H (2013) A unified framework for 3d hand tracking. In: International symposium on visual computing. Springer, pp 129–139
33. Tang D, Jin Chang H, Tejani A, Kim T-K (2014) Latent regression forest: Structured estimation of 3d articulated hand posture. In: Proceedings of the IEEE conference on computer vision and pattern recognition, pp 3786–3793
34. Tompson J, Stein M, Lecun Y, Perlin K (2014) Real-time continuous pose recovery of human hands using convolutional networks. ACM Trans Graphics (ToG) 33(5):1–10
35. Taylor GW, Sigal L, Fleet DJ, Hinton GE (2010) Dynamical binary latent variable models for 3d human pose tracking. In: 2010 IEEE computer society conference on computer vision and pattern recognition. IEEE, pp 631–638
36. Hafiz AR, Al-Nuaimi AY, Amin M, Murase K et al (2015) Classification of skeletal wireframe representation of hand gesture using complex-valued neural network. Neural Process Lett 42(3):649–664
37. Toshev A, Szegedy C (2014) Deeppose: human pose estimation via deep neural networks. In: Proceedings of the IEEE conference on computer vision and pattern recognition, pp 1653–1660
38. Tompson JJ, Jain A, LeCun Y, Bregler C (2014) Joint training of a convolutional network and a graphical model for human pose estimation. In: Advances in neural information processing systems, vol 27
39. Sinha A, Choi C, Ramani K (2016) Deephand: robust hand pose estimation by completing a matrix imputed with deep features. In: Proceedings of the IEEE conference on computer vision and pattern recognition, pp 4150–4158
40. Oberweger M, Wohlhart P, Lepetit V (2015) Hands deep in deep learning for hand pose estimation. arXiv:1502.06807
41. Neverova N, Wolf C, Nebout F, Taylor GW (2017) Hand pose estimation through semi-supervised and weakly-supervised learning. Comput Vis Image Underst 164:56–67
42. Ge L, Liang H, Yuan J, Thalmann D (2016) Robust 3d hand pose estimation in single depth images: from single-view cnn to multi-view cnns. In: Proceedings of the IEEE conference on computer vision and pattern recognition, pp 3593–3601
43. Hinton GE, Osindero S, Teh Y-W (2006) A fast learning algorithm for deep belief nets. Neural Comput 18(7):1527–1554
44. LeCun Y, Bottou L, Bengio Y, Haffner P (1998) Gradient-based learning applied to document recognition. Proc IEEE 86(11):2278–2324
45. Hsu R-L, Abdel-Mottaleb M, Jain AK (2002) Face detection in colorimages. IEEE Trans Pattern Anal Mach Intell 24(5):696–706
46. Maas AL, Hannun AY, Ng AY et al (2013) Rectifier nonlinearities improve neural network acoustic models. In: Proceedings of ICML, vol 30. Citeseer, p 3

47. Wong SC, Gatt A, Stamatescu V, McDonnell MD (2016) Understanding data augmentation for classification: when to warp? In: 2016 International conference on digital image computing: techniques and applications (DICTA). IEEE, pp 1–6
48. Szegedy C, Liu W, Jia Y, Sermanet P, Reed S, Anguelov D, Erhan D, Vanhoucke V, Rabinovich A (2015) Going deeper with convolutions. In: Proceedings of the IEEE conference on computer vision and pattern recognition, pp 1–9
49. Szegedy C, Vanhoucke V, Ioffe S, Shlens J, Wojna Z (2016) Rethinking the inception architecture for computer vision. In: Proceedings of the IEEE conference on computer vision and pattern recognition, pp 2818–2826
50. Szegedy C, Ioffe S, Vanhoucke V, Alemi AA (2017) Inception-v4, inception-resnet and the impact of residual connections on learning. In: Thirty-first AAAI conference on artificial intelligence
51. Hu Z, Hu Y, Wu B, Liu J, Han D, Kurfess T (2018) Hand pose estimation with multi-scale network. Appl Intell 48(8):2501–2515
52. Ji S, Xu W, Yang M, Yu K (2012) 3d convolutional neural networks for human action recognition. IEEE Trans Pattern Anal Mach Intell 35(1):221–231
53. Tran D, Bourdev L, Fergus R, Torresani L, Paluri M (2015) Learning spatiotemporal features with 3d convolutional networks. In: Proceedings of the IEEE international conference on computer vision, pp 4489–4497
54. Molchanov P, Gupta S, Kim K, Kautz J (2015) Hand gesture recognition with 3d convolutional neural networks. In: Proceedings of the IEEE conference on computer vision and pattern recognition workshops, pp 1–7
55. Molchanov P, Yang X, Gupta S, Kim K, Tyree S, Kautz J (2016) Online detection and classification of dynamic hand gestures with recurrent 3d convolutional neural network. In: Proceedings of the IEEE conference on computer vision and pattern recognition, pp 4207–4215
56. Donahue J, Anne Hendricks L, Guadarrama S, Rohrbach M, Venugopalan S, Saenko K, Darrell T (2015) Long-term recurrent convolutional networks for visual recognition and description. In: Proceedings of the IEEE conference on computer vision and pattern recognition, pp 2625–2634
57. Yue-Hei Ng J, Hauschknecht M, Vijayanarasimhan S, Vinyals O, Monga R, Toderici G (2015) Beyond short snippets: deep networks for video classification. In: Proceedings of the IEEE conference on computer vision and pattern recognition, pp 4694–4702
58. Simonyan K, Zisserman A (2014) Two-stream convolutional networks for action recognition in videos. In: Advances in neural information processing systems, vol 27
59. Feichtenhofer C, Pinz A, Zisserman A (2016) Convolutional two-stream network fusion for video action recognition. In: Proceedings of the IEEE conference on computer vision and pattern recognition, pp 1933–1941
60. Ma C-Y, Chen M-H, Kira Z, AlRegib G (2019) TS-LSTM and temporal-inception: exploiting spatiotemporal dynamics for activity recognition. Signal Process: Image Commun 71:76–87
61. Pei M, Wu X, Guo Y, Fujita H (2017) Small bowel motility assessment based on fully convolutional networks and long short-term memory. Knowl-Based Syst 121:163–172
62. Moni M, Ali AS (2009) Hmm based hand gesture recognition: a review on techniques and approaches. In: 2009 2nd IEEE international conference on computer science and information technology. IEEE, pp 433–437
63. Rossi M, Benatti S, Farella E, Benini L (2015) Hybrid EMG classifier based on hmm and svm for hand gesture recognition in prosthetics. In: 2015 IEEE international conference on industrial technology (ICIT). IEEE, pp 1700–1705
64. Saha S, Bhattacharya S, Konar A (2018) A novel approach to gesture recognition in sign language applications using AVL tree and SVM. In: Progress in intelligent computing techniques: theory, practice, and applications. Springer, pp 271–277
65. Yun L, Peng Z (2009) An automatic hand gesture recognition system based on viola-jones method and svms. In: 2009 Second international workshop on computer science and engineering, vol 2. IEEE, pp 72–76
66. Elmezain M, Al-Hamadi A, Michaelis B (2010) A robust method for hand gesture segmentation and recognition using forward spotting scheme in conditional random fields. In: 2010 20th International conference on pattern recognition. IEEE, pp 3850–3853

67. Diba A, Pazandeh AM, Van Gool L (2016) Efficient two-stream motion and appearance 3d cnns for video classification. arXiv:1608.08851
68. Ma C-Y, Chen M-H, Kira Z, AlRegib G (2019) Ts-lstm and temporalinception: exploiting spatiotemporal dynamics for activity recognition. Signal Process: Image Commun 71:76–87
69. Han S, Mao H, Dally WJ (2015) Deep compression: compressing deep neural networks with pruning, trained quantization and huffman coding. arXiv:1510.00149
70. Rastegari M, Ordonez V, Redmon J, Farhadi A (2016) Xnor-net: Imagenet classification using binary convolutional neural networks. In: European conference on computer vision. Springer, pp 525–542
71. Hinton G, Vinyals O, Dean J et al (2015) Distilling the knowledge in a neural network. 2(7). arXiv:1503.02531
72. Howard AG, Zhu M, Chen B, Kalenichenko D, Wang W, Weyand T, Andreetto M, Adam H (2017) Mobilenets: efficient convolutional neural networks for mobile vision applications. arXiv:1704.04861
73. Iandola FN, Han S, Moskewicz MW, Ashraf K, Dally WJ, Keutzer K (2016) Squeezenet: Alexnet-level accuracy with $50\times$ fewer parameters and ¡ 0.5 mb model size. arXiv:1602.07360

Chapter 3
Vision-Based Facial Activity Recognition

Abstract This chapter introduces the facial-related explicit activities using the low-cost camera, including head pose estimation and tracking, gaze direction estimation, and gaze fixation tracking. The facial activities are important cues that can indicate human attention and intention, which are the key technique to construct the harmonious human–machine system. The corresponding data-driven DL-based approaches are introduced and analysed. The corresponding available datasets are introduced for the related researcher reference. Leveraging the advanced deep learning approach, the existing studies have achieved outstanding performance. In the future, we encourage the researchers can put attention to the collection of large and accurate datasets that can unify the facial states.

3.1 Introduction

The human face is the most informative area and plays an essential role in social communication. The face can be used to identify species, lip-read what is said, and understand someone's emotional state and intentions based on the displayed facial expression [1]. The expression on a person's face can also reveal their personality, attractiveness, age, and gender. Human face-to-face communication is an excellent model for developing a multi-modal human–machine interface. It can inspire us when developing the related application and give us some clues. Due to its importance, it has attracted numerous researchers to study it from various perspectives. A plethora of promising technologies have been created. The most successful technique is the face recognition systems, which can match a face from a digital database, are commonly used to authenticate users through identity verification services in a variety of applications and scenarios, including the smartphone unlock, security monitoring, digital payment, etc. Many entertainment applications are also developed based on it, such as the cartoon avatar generation, dynamic facial expression generation, camera relighting, etc. The face recognition technology is an inextricably linked part of our lives.

The facial-related activity can be basically classified into two categories: explicit activity and implicit activity. The implicit one mainly involves the psychological state of the human. One of the typical topics is affective computing [2], which aims to study and develop a system that can recognize, interpret, process, and simulate human emotional states. It is a multidisciplinary topic that includes computer science, psychology, and cognitive science, which is a vivid research field that has attracted considerable attention. The common approach is to analyse the facial image because the facial expression is the most related clue for the emotional state. The affective computing, on the other hand, could gather clues from a variety of sources, including posture, gestures, speech, and others that can all signify changes in the user's emotional state and be detected and interpreted. The development of computer vision and deep learning technology has promoted its progress, which can extract meaningful patterns from the gathered multi-modal data. The other typical study is the intention prediction, which attempts to infer the human's intention under certain situations. It is a crucial task to construct harmonious human–machine systems, especially for the automated vehicle, which can provide the necessary assistance according to the driver's intention and increase the user experience [3]. Usually, it relies on explicit activity recognition as well as the contextual perception. The explicit activity mainly includes two research objects: head [4, 5]and eyes [6]. The head pose is an important cue that can reflect the human's attention state and further infer the intention, which is widely used to recognize the human distraction, driver attention, lane change intention, etc. It is also necessary fundamental information to build the immersive virtual reality application, where the virtual viewpoint must align with the head pose. The famous phrase "eyes are the window to the soul" refers to the idea that you can understand his or her emotions and sometimes thoughts by looking into a person's eyes. It reveals that the eye's activity is an important feature that contains much information in the interaction. There are two common tasks associated with it: gaze direction estimation and gaze fixation estimation, both of which can provide significant information to aid in the inference of the human attention state. The recognition of facial-related activity in intelligent agents could enrich and facilitate interactivity between humans and machines (Fig. 3.1).

There are various devices and sensors that can capture facial-related activity, such as gaze tracker glasses, head tracking sensor, other physiological sensors. However, these devices adopt an intrusive manner, which will reduce the acceptance of the user. In comparison, this book prefers non-intrusive visual sensors, especially the low-cost vision camera. Due to explicit activities being more easily precepted from human appearance states, they are also the fundamental information that can support the

Fig. 3.1 The taxonomy of the facial-related activity

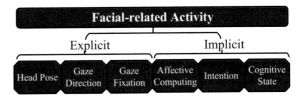

inference of implicit activity. Therefore, this chapter will more focus on the explicit activity's recognition based on the visual approach.

3.2 Appearance-Based Head Pose Estimation

Head pose as a crucial clue has contained much information that can indicate the human's attention and intention, which has been utilized in many human–machine systems. Many human-related tasks, such as gaze detection, driver attention, human behaviour analysis, and fatigue detection, require high accuracy and robustness in head pose estimation. It can also be used to enhance the method performance in some face-related tasks, such as expression detection and identity recognition. The immersion of virtual reality also relies on the correct estimation of the user's head pose to obtain the synchronized view rendering.

There are a variety of sensors available for estimating head pose, including RGB, depth, infrared (IR), inertial measurement unit (IMU), and optical marker. Users are more accepting of the non-intrusive approach based on the visual sensor. The advancement of computer vision technology has also led to an increase in the number of researchers adopting vision-based approach. Head pose estimation is a task that requires deducing 3D information about the head from input data. A naïve idea is to employ a depth sensor to obtain 3D data of the head [7, 8]. Several geometry-based methods [9, 10] fit a single RGB or depth face image using a predefined 3D facial model. The essence of geometry-based methods is to make use of prior knowledge about the head shape, which is formed as a registration optimization task. Its most important step is to obtain accurate feature matching. The first idea is to use the facial landmark to obtain high-quality 2D facial features, whilst the second is to optimize or augment a predefined 3D model. Geometry-based methods, as a result, are frequently a combination of multiple approaches, and they require a predefined 3D model and combine some landmark-based methods which are frequently necessary to rely on the facial landmark detection model [11, 12]. Some studies directly utilize these landmarks to infer the head pose, whilst others integrate them into their own models to improve the model performance. The issue is that the ground truth of the face landmark is time-consuming. We prefer to introduce the landmark-free method in this chapter. Most of the existing solutions have one thing in common: they make use of additional information, which, on the other hand, comes at a cost. As a result, the goal of this chapter is to introduce a low-cost solution to estimate head pose based on a single 2D image.

The output of head pose estimation is generally divided into two categories: direct regression [13] and converting to a classification problem, also known as a "soft label problem" [14–17]. When the estimation output is converted into a classification problem, the image as a whole is considered, so it is often necessary to preprocess the image first and crop out the head area; otherwise, training the model is difficult. When CNN is first applied, human pose estimation also directly regresses the coordinates of joint points. Then heatmaps are widely used in the methods of the human body pose estimation [18]. The basic idea is that each joint point corresponds to a single heatmap. The advantage of this method is that the output includes classification as well as regression. The classification is divided into two levels: classifying the various heatmaps that distinguish the various joint points and classifying the foreground and background in a single heatmap. In a sense, the regression of the position of the joint point is a classification problem; that is, the pixel value on the heatmap indicates the probability that it belongs to a joint point, which can be thought of as a 2D version of one-hot encoding which is commonly used for classification tasks. This section will introduce a novel output, the Bernoulli heatmap, that can achieve a fully convolutional network for head pose estimation, focusing the network on the head area. The proposed Bernoulli heatmap value follows the Bernoulli distribution rather than the Gaussian distribution, and the final estimate is the average of non-zero values. From some perspectives, it combines the two tasks of head detection and pose regression, so preprocessing of the head crop is not required.

3.2.1 End-To-End Head Pose Estimation Model

1. Bernoulli Heatmap

Spatial generalization is a critical capability in computer vision tasks, particularly coordinate regression. Convolutional layers, in general, have spatial ability due to weight sharing, but fully connected layers are prone to overfitting, limiting the overall network's spatial generalization ability [19]. Gaussian heatmaps are the most used method in the field of human pose estimation, which can convert the overall network into a fully convolutional network without the fully connected layer, allowing for a larger feature map with better spatial generalization. It is easier for the network to converge because it is no longer required to convert spatial information into coordinate information on its own.

The Gaussian heatmap, on the other hand, has two flaws. (1) The coordinate regression problem has a lower bound of theoretical error because its output is an integer. There is a calculation error when the output map is reduced by n times the original image. The error increases as n increases. (2) The Gaussian heatmap employs the MSE loss function, which may result in an offset, as illustrated in Fig. 3.2. When the loss is low, it does not imply that the prediction is more accurate; however, there may be some deviations. Head pose estimation is regressed not only to joint point coordinates but also to three angles about head rotation. As a result, the Gaussian heatmap cannot be directly used. The Bernoulli heatmap is introduced as a solution to tackle this task, and different angles correspond to different Bernoulli heatmaps. The ground truth of position p of the ith Bernoulli heatmap is defined as $L_i(p)$:

$$L_i(p) = \begin{cases} v & \text{if } p \text{ in the } c \\ 0 & \text{otherwise} \end{cases} \tag{3.1}$$

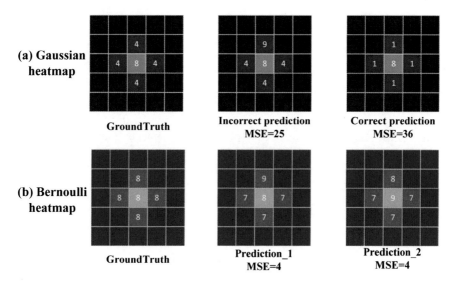

Fig. 3.2 Illustration of the Gaussian heatmap (**a**) and Bernoulli heatmap (**b**)

where v is the value of the ith angle, and c is a circle whose centre is the centre of the head area with a radius r which is a hyperparameter.

During testing, the angle L_i is

$$L_i = \frac{1}{n(p)} \sum L_i(p) \qquad (3.2)$$

where $n(p)$ is the mean number of non-zero $L_i(p)$. The Bernoulli heatmap still induces the model focus on the head area but is unconcerned about the exact centre head point coordinates, so theoretical error lower bounds and deviations are not an issue.

The receptive field is a critical component of the convolutional neural network. The value of each convolutional layer output node is determined by a specific area of the convolutional layer's input. Other input values outside of this range have no effect on the output value. The classic object detection utilizes a region proposal network (RPN), where the anchor is the basis of the RPN, and the receptive field is the basis of the anchor. The theory of effective receptive field (ERF) was proposed in [20]. They discovered that not all pixels in the receptive field contribute equally to the output vector or feature map. In many cases, the effective pixels of the receptive field conform to the Gaussian distribution, which only occupies a portion of the theoretical receptive field and rapidly decays from the centre to the edge. This also implies that the predictability of each pixel on the Bernoulli heatmap varies. The closer to the head region, the higher the reliability, and the farther away from the head region, the lower the reliability. As a result, in addition to the Bernoulli heatmap, the final output of the model includes a Gaussian heatmap, which represents the probability of different positions away from the centre of the head and thus the weights of different positions. The final estimation formula is as follows:

$$L_i = \frac{1}{\sum w_p} \sum w_p * L_i(p), w_p \sim N(\mu, \sigma^2) \tag{3.3}$$

where w_p is the corresponding weight on the Gaussian heatmap, μ is the centre of the head area, and μ affects the heatmap's weight distribution. In this section, L_i is set to 0.6 *r. The goal is to reduce the effective area of the Gaussian heatmap to that of the Bernoulli heatmap. Only pixels with w_p greater than 0.5 are used for the calculations in the experiments. The radius r is important in the receptive field, particularly the ERF. It is obvious that when the head area is included in the receptive field, the angle is predicted; otherwise, it is 0. This is the same as cropping the input image inside the network, including the head region as positive samples and the rest as negative samples.

2. Network Architecture
Many existing pose estimation networks are built in series from high-to-low resolution subnetworks, with each subnetwork consisting of a sequence of convolution layers and a down-sample layer to achieve low resolution. These methods must recover high-resolution representations from low-resolution representations. Recently, the HRNet has outperformed the competition, which is successful in two ways: (1) maintaining high-resolution representations across the network without recovering high resolution from low resolution representations; and (2) repeatedly fusing multi-resolution representations, resulting in reliable high-resolution representations. As a result, we can use this multi-scale/multi-resolution representation as our foundation, as shown in Fig. 3.3. The network is divided into four stages, each with its own set of subnetworks. The subnetwork is made up of various numbers of Bottleneck or BasicBlock modules. These modules are made up of several convolutional layers, batch normalization layers, and activation layers. The Transition module is used to down-sample and add branches as the next stage's input. It is believed that the key capability of the convolution network is the ability to learn different levels of features that contribute differently to the output vector. In general, the current fusion is the addition of equal weights. However, we hope that their weights can be learned during feature map fusion.

Inspired by the work of Zhang et al. [21], we trained the network to fuse multi-scale feature maps and exploit the interdependencies between feature channels. The channel-wise fusion technique is used as shown in Fig. 3.4. Let $X = [x_1, ..., x_c.., x_C]$ be the feature maps of one branch before fusion, with C feature maps of size $H \times W$. The c-th weight of w is then determined by

$$w_c = f\left(W_2 * \delta\left(W_1 * \frac{\sum_{i=1}^{H} \sum_{j=1}^{W} x_c(i,j)}{H \times W}\right)\right) \tag{3.4}$$

$$\widehat{x_c} = (1 + w_c) \cdot x_c \tag{3.5}$$

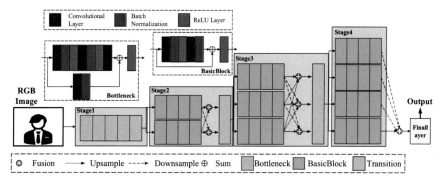

Fig. 3.3 The architecture of the multi-resolution model for the head pose estimation

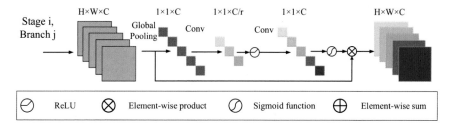

Fig. 3.4 Illustration of the channel-wise fusion

where $x_c(i, j)$ is the value of the c-th feature x_c at position (i, j). As can be seen, global average pooling (GAP) is performed first, which can be thought of as the aggregation of local descriptors to express the entire information. The weight set of a convolution layer as channel-downscaling with reduction ratio r is denoted by W_1.

The W_2 is the weight set of the channel-upscaling layer with r, where $f()$ and $\delta()$ are the sigmoid and ReLU activation functions, respectively. The activation functions can derive the channel-wise dependencies from the aggregated vector, and then the non-linear interactions between channels and the non-mutually exclusive relationship can be learned, allowing multiple channel-wise features to be emphasized rather than one-hot activation. The final channel weights w_c are then obtained and utilized to rescale the feature map x_c, where w_c and x_c are the scaling factor and feature map in the c-th channel, respectively.

3.2.2 Model Analysis

1. Datasets

There are three popular head pose datasets: BIWI [22], AFLW2000 [23], and 300 W-LP [23], each of which contains a real image with 3D pose angles. In addition, 300W-LP contains a synthesized image with the pose angles. Because the BIWI dataset is made up entirely of real images, it can be used as the primary dataset to discuss the introduced method. However, AFLW2000 can be used as a supplementary test set.

The BIWI is made up of 24 sequences captured with a Kinect sensor. Twenty people (six women and fourteen men were recorded twice) were recorded whilst turning their heads and sitting in front of the sensor at about one meter. There are nearly 15,000 images in the database, with yaw angles of 75°, pitch angles of 60°, and roll angles of 50°.

The 300W across Large Poses (300W-LP) database contains 61,225 synthesized face samples from multiple alignment databases, including AFW, LFPW, HELEN, and IBUG, which were then flipped to 122,450 samples. There are several synthesized pose faces with varying degrees of yaw for each original image. The AFLW2000 database contains the first 2000 AFLW samples' ground-truth 3D faces and the corresponding 68 landmarks. The samples in the dataset have a wide range of poses with varying lighting and expressions.

2. Network Setting
The network is divided into four stages, as shown in Fig. 3.3, with each stage having a different number of subnetworks. The subnetwork is made up of various numbers of Bottlenecks or BasicBlocks, as shown in Table 3.1. The NUM CHANNELS value corresponds to the channel number of each bottleneck or BasicBlock module. The multi-step learning rate decay was used. INITIAL VALUE is the initial learning rate, LR FACTOR is a learning rate decay multiplicative factor, and LR STEP is a list of epoch indices. Aside from the sigmoid activation function used in channel-wise fusion, the other activation functions were leaky ReLU with a leaky value of 0.2. The Adam optimizer was adopted during training.

Two types of evaluation criteria were adopted to evaluate the estimation results. Criterion I: The MAE between estimation and ground truth for each angle in the test set, which can provide a macroscopic assessment of the result. Criterion II: The proportion of all three angles in all samples is less than a certain value. This criterion is more microscopic than the first and is concerned with local bad estimations.

To compare with others, the 16 videos of the BIWI dataset were utilized for training and the remaining 8 videos for testing. We conducted several sets of experiments to investigate the effect of the hyperparameter r as shown in Fig. 3.5. The AT stands for channel-wise fusion, the BG denotes a situation with a background, the nBG denotes a situation without a background. The first group of experiments shows that the network has channel-wise fusion with different r whilst the second group shows that the network does not have channel-wise fusion. It is clear that the r has an impact on the estimation results. When the r was too large, the effective receptive field of some effective pixels on the heatmap did not contain valid head information, implying that the "negative sample" was regarded as a "positive sample," resulting in large errors. Similarly, when the was r too small, some "positive samples" were mislabelled as "negative samples," which also inevitably led to errors.

When the basic parameters are the same, the channel-wise fusion benefits the model, as shown in Figs. 3.5 and 3.6. When the error threshold is less than 3, the slope of the curve is large, and the accuracy is greater than 50% at this time, after

Table 3.1 The utilized hyperparameters

Testing	BIWI	
	With background	Without background
Input size	128 × 96	64 × 64
Stage1	NUM_BOTTLENECK	NUM_CHANNELS
	4	64
Stage2	4	32
	4	64
Stage3	4	32
	4	64
	4	128
Stage4	4	32
	4	64
	4	128
	4	256
Learning rate	Initial value	0.001
	LR_FACTOR	0.5
	LR_STEP	15
		30

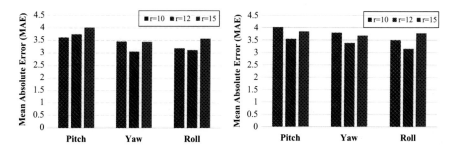

Fig. 3.5 The comparisons of different hyperparameter in r case of **Criterion I**: HR-AT-nBG (left) and HR-nBG (right)

which the slope gradually decreases. When the threshold is around 5, the accuracy percentage is around 80%. This means that our methods have a lower overall error, but the presence of a small number of samples with larger errors raises the average error.

Furthermore, the translation and occlusion of the test set were used to test the robustness of the introduced method without retraining the model. Each case was tested five times, whilst the test sample being processed at random each time, and the results can be found in Fig. 3.7. The MAE increased slightly when there was some occlusion and translation, but not significantly. It can be considered that the model

Fig. 3.6 The comparisons
of different hyperparameter
r in case of *Criterion II*

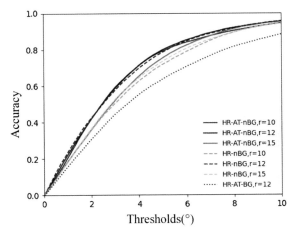

Fig. 3.7 The comparison
with different processing of
test set

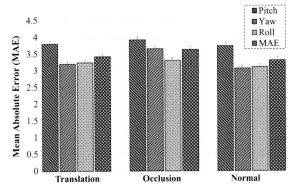

will be able to handle more severe translation and occlusion problems by augmenting
the training samples.

The most important feature of neural networks is generalization. There are three
protocols that are utilized to assess the generalization of the introduced method.
Protocol 1: As previously described, 16 videos (10,000 frames) from the BIWI dataset
were used for training, with the remaining 8 videos (5000 frames) used for testing.
Protocol 2: The BIWI dataset was divided into 12 videos (7500 frames) for training
and 12 videos (7500 frames) for testing. Protocol 3: The BIWI dataset was used for
training with approximately 8 videos (5000 frames), and the remaining 16 videos
(10,000 frames) were used for testing. Generally, when there were more training
samples, the error was lower. When there were few training samples, the test results
remained within a reasonable range as shown in Fig. 3.8. This demonstrates that the
introduced method has a reasonable generalizable, and better results can be obtained
as the training sample size increased.

Fig. 3.8 The comparison of different protocols

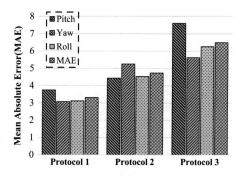

3.2.3 Summary

This section has introduced an appearance-based head pose estimation approach with a novel Bernoulli heatmap, which transforms the network into a fully convolutional network and provides a new idea for head pose estimation. The Bernoulli heatmap not only regresses the head angles, but it also allows the network to distinguish between the foreground and the background, which can improve the network's robustness. This will benefit the integration of human pose estimation to form an end-to-end whole-body pose estimation. To maintain high-resolution representations, a network structure with multi-scale representations is utilized, which is similar to the HRNet. The distinction is that channel-wise fusion is leveraged, which allows the fusion weights of feature maps with varying resolutions to be learned. Experiments show that the introduced can achieve the state-of-the-art performance in public dataset, and it can be further improved using more diversity samples.

3.3 Dynamic Head Tracking System

To determine the human activity state, head pose estimation can be applied to a variety of human–machine systems. A typical application is the simulation platform, in which the head pose is the key enabling technique that can improve the system's immersion. Intelligent driving is a current hot research field that necessitates the collaboration of multiple disciplines and algorithms. Developing and testing algorithms in real-world intelligent vehicles is a costly and time-consuming process. The advancement of simulation technology provides an alternative path; the simulator can provide physically and visually realistic simulation for a variety of research goals, as well as collect many annotated samples to leverage deep learning and machine learning [24]. The cockpit of a driving simulator is a popular experimental platform. The immersion is one of the key features. One approach to improving visual realism is to use VR devices; however, this introduces two issues: (1) Dizziness caused by a significant mismatch between the fixed seat and the dynamic virtual graphic; (2)

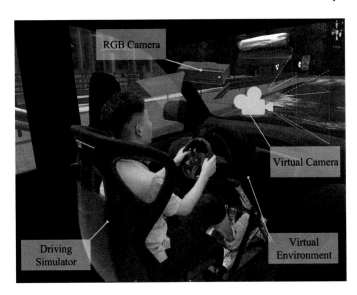

Fig. 3.9 The driving simulator with head tracking system, which includes the input devices, computing server, and RGB camera

The VR glasses will cover the driver's face, making research on the driver's state impossible [25]. As a result, the goal of this section is to introduce a vision-based driver head tracking system to improve immersion and interaction, as illustrated in Fig. 3.9. This technique can also be used to improve the user experience of intelligent vehicles' head-up display and other driver-in-the-loop applications.

The previous studies primarily made use of specialized devices or sensors. Sim et al. [26] proposed a wearable head-tracking device with inertial sensors as an indicator of human movement intentions for Brain–Machine Interface applications. Kang et al. [27] presented a sensor fusion method that incorporates the IMU, IR, RGB camera, and other sensors. Ng et al. [28] created a low-cost head tracking device for virtual reality systems based on the SteamVR Tracking technology. To build the head tracking system, these methods typically use a variety of sensors. There are also several similar products in the flight simulator field, which usually require a special device or optical marker, such as an infrared camera. Although some devices only require the RGB camera, all of them require the user to manually adjust the relative parameters, and they typically use some traditional head estimation methods. As a result, the goal of this section is to introduce a low-cost and mark-free solution that relies solely on the RGB sensor as an input device, whilst a dynamic head pose estimation model based on deep learning is developed to improve the accuracy of the system.

To achieve the state-of-the-art performance, many different types of head pose estimation models combined with multiple modalities input are currently proposed. These methods are classified as model-based or model-free. To fit the input image, model-based methods typically employ a deformable head model. They must also locate the facial landmarks to align the predefined model. These methods are typically time-consuming. Model-free approaches are more popular, in which a regression model is trained to map the head image to the pose manifold, and deep learning-based models are primarily used as described in the previous section. Facial landmarks are also used in some model-free research to estimate the head pose and can be used with vision geometry algorithms or multi-task learning to improve model performance [29]. To eliminate the influence of illumination intensity, the depth image is investigated to obtain more robust head poses in low-light or high-light variation conditions. The depth image can also provide additional depth information to improve the model's accuracy. These methods essentially estimate the head pose for each frame independently. As a dynamic head tracker, this section will concentrate on leveraging the prior frame to improve the model's performance. The RNN is a popular model for dealing with sequential data, and it can be combined with the CNN to handle video-based tasks. Recently, self-attention-based models, particularly vision transformers, have demonstrated significant potential in a variety of tasks [30]. Based on the massive dataset, they outperform inductive bias methods such as CNN and RNN models. However, these transformers typically only focus on the image's spatial information or the temporal feature of the sequential data. As a result, this section introduces a novel spatial-temporal vision transformer structure.

Usually, the estimated curve of consecutive frames will fluctuate due to the model's error variance. As part of the post-processing, the Kalman Filter is used to address this issue. By analysing the estimation model's error distribution, an adaptive Kalman Filter (AKF) is utilized to improve filtering performance, which includes an adaptive observation noise coefficient and can adaptively moderate smoothness and keep the curve stable near the initial position.

3.3.1 Vision-Based Driver Head Pose Tracker

A well-established vision-based dynamic head tracker for the driving simulator requires the virtual view can be automatically aligned with the driver's head pose via a frontal RGB camera. The advantages are as follows: (1) It can improve the simulator's immersion and interaction. The driver's view will be unrestricted and non-fixed, and the virtual camera will be synchronized with the driver's head pose; (2) The extracted head pose can also be used to monitor the driver's state; and (3) It is a low-cost solution via a non-invasive camera sensor.

The advancement of deep learning and computer vision technology provides the fundamental support. The currently state-of-the-art head pose estimation methods typically use a single frame as input. In this section, the prior frame will be utilized along with the current frame to improve the model's performance. To address this problem, a novel spatial-temporal vision transformer is introduced, and the AKF is adopted to smooth the estimation's inconsistency and volatility. The overall architecture is shown in Fig. 3.10.

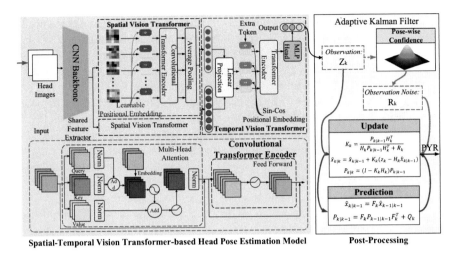

Spatial-Temporal Vision Transformer-based Head Pose Estimation Model   **Post-Processing**

Fig. 3.10 The framework of introduced spatial-temporal vision transformer model, which is adopted as the measurer to estimate the pose, and its result as the observation. An adaptive Kalman Filter is used to optimize the estimation

3.3.1.1   Dynamic Head Pose Estimation

With the advancement of deep learning, research on head pose estimation has also yielded promising results, but they typically use a single frame as input. To improve the model performance, the prior frame can be leveraged combined with the current frame as an input pair. Typically, RNN is a widely used model for dealing with this type of sequential data, and it can use CNN as a feature extractor to deal with video-based tasks. It is worth noting that the transformer model has demonstrated enormous potential, particularly in natural language processing (NLP). Some researchers have begun to apply it to computer vision tasks, proposing vision transformer models [30]. In comparison to inductive bias models such as CNN and RNN, the transformer can handle large amounts of data and achieve better performance on large datasets.

The section introduces a spatial-temporal vision transformer (ST-ViT) architecture to address the dynamic driver head pose, as shown in the left of Fig. 3.10. The input pair consists of two loosely cropped images from a face detector, which allows the model to focus on the head area and is simple to train. The ST-ViT still employs a CNN backbone as the feature extractor, as opposed to the pure vision transformer method, which requires a massive dataset to train. The weight of the feature extractor is shared between the input pairs. The extracted feature maps will be used by the spatial vision transformer module. The positional embedding is learnable in this module, and the transformer encoder is convolutional, which computes the Query, Key, and Value via the convolutional layer rather than the linear connection layer, as shown below:

$$\begin{cases} Q_{(u,v)} = \mathrm{BN}\big(\mathrm{Conv}(x, W_Q)\big) = BN\left(\sum_i \sum_j wq_{u-i,v-j} \cdot x_{i,j}\right) \\[2em] K_{(u,v)} = \mathrm{BN}(\mathrm{Conv}(x, W_K)) = \mathrm{BN}\left(\sum_i \sum_j wk_{u-i,v-j} \cdot x_{i,j}\right) \\[2em] V_{(u,v)} = \mathrm{BN}(\mathrm{Conv}(x, W_V)) = \mathrm{BN}\left(\sum_i \sum_j wv_{u-i,v-j} \cdot x_{i,j}\right) \end{cases} \quad (3.6)$$

where BN denotes the batch normalization layer, Conv indicates the convolutional layer without bias, and W represents the weight kernel. The QKV will then be used by the multi-head attention mechanism to extract the multiple semantic information as follows:

$$\begin{aligned} x_{\mathrm{out}} &= \mathrm{Conv}_{\mathrm{out}}(\mathrm{Attention}(Q, K, V)) \\ &= \mathrm{Conv}_{\mathrm{out}}\left(\mathrm{softmax}\left(\frac{QK^T + \mathrm{Pos}}{\sqrt{d_k}}\right)V\right) \end{aligned} \quad (3.7)$$

where Pos is the learnable position bias and d_k is the dimension of the Key. The dependency and relationship of the feature maps of a single image can be obtained using the convolutional attention module and the two convolutional forward layers. The temporal vision transformer (T-ViT) will receive the image pair's feature vectors via an average pooling layer, and the feature vectors will be embedded via a linear projection layer. The positional embedding is fixed in this module, which uses the sin-cos function, as shown in Eq. 3.8, to compute the position encoding, and an extra token is used to concatenate with the embedding vector, which is designed to predict the last frame through the final MLP Head.

$$\begin{cases} \mathrm{PE}_{(\mathrm{pos},2i)} = \sin\big(\mathrm{pos}/10000^{2i/d_{\mathrm{vector}}}\big) \\ \mathrm{PE}_{(\mathrm{pos},2i+1)} = \cos\big(\mathrm{pos}/10000^{2i/d_{\mathrm{vector}}}\big) \end{cases} \quad (3.8)$$

2. Adaptive Kalman Filter

Although the current head pose estimation method performs well, there is still some error. Its flaws of fluctuation and discontinuity will be highlighted when applied to the simulator. In practice, the smoothness and consistency of the view changes are more important than the accuracy. The Kalman Filter (KF) is an algorithm that provides estimates of some unknown variables, given the measurements observed over time and contained statistical noise and other inaccuracies. The KFs have been shown to be useful in a variety of applications, including vehicle guidance, navigation, and control. It has a simple design and requires few computational resources.

To use the KF, the problem must be modelled, and it is assumed to be a linear model to ensure real-time performance. Assume that the posterior state estimation of the head pose at k time is $\hat{x}_{k|k}$. The prediction phase is as follows:

$$\begin{cases} \hat{x}_{k|k-1} = F_k \hat{x}_{k-1|k-1} \\ P_{k|k-1} = F_k P_{k-1|k-1} F_k^T + Q_k \\ F_k = \begin{bmatrix} I_{3\times3} & \Delta t \cdot I_{3\times3} \\ 0 & I_{3\times3} \end{bmatrix} \end{cases} \tag{3.9}$$

where $\hat{x}_{k|k-1}$ means the prior state estimation, $\hat{x}_{k|k-1}$ represents the state-transition matrix, $P_{k|k-1}$ denotes the prior state estimation covariance at k time, whilst the $P_{k-1|k-1}$ is the posterior estimation covariance at $k-1$ time. Q_k means the process noise. The $I_{3\times3}$ represents the identity matrix of 3×3 size. Then the update phase is:

$$\begin{cases} K_k = \dfrac{P_{k|k-1} H_k^T}{H_k P_{k|k-1} H_k^T + R_k} \\ \hat{x}_{k|k} = \hat{x}_{k|k-1} + K_k\left(z_k - H_k \hat{x}_{k|k-1}\right) \\ P_{k|k} = (I - K_k H_k) P_{k|k-1} \end{cases} \tag{3.10}$$

where K_k denotes the Kalman gain factor, H_k means the measurement matrix which converts the state variable into the corresponding observation variable. The $\hat{x}_{k|k}$ is the posterior state estimation, which is also the pose of the virtual camera of the simulator. The z_k is the output of the head pose estimation model, which as the observation value. The $P_{k|k}$ is the posterior estimation covariance at k time. The R_k is the observation noise covariance, which is related to the estimation model and will also affect the performance of the filter.

To determine the R_k, the results of the head pose estimation model are studied. Through statistics, it is found that the model usually has different performances in different intervals of the head pose. When the pose angle is small, the accuracy is higher; otherwise, the error is greater, especially on the Pitch and Roll axes. As a result, this section introduces an adaptive R_k, which can be adjusted adaptively during the iterative process. When the rotation angle is small, it can bring the filtered value close to the observed value, whilst when the rotation angle is large, the filtered value changes more smoothly.

3.3.2 Model Analysis

The BIWI dataset is used to evaluate the introduced method due to it provides the videos. The other datasets lack sequential images. In this section, the EfficientNet-b0 is used to extract the feature maps. It is a popular backbone that develops a new baseline network by performing a neural architecture search and optimizes both accuracy and efficiency.

Four paradigms are designed to validate the proposed method: (1) **Baseline** A MLP is used to tackle the extracted feature maps from the CNN backbone, with 512 hidden neurons. (2) **LSTM** In comparison to Baseline, the image pair is used as the input rather than a single image, and the image pair is handled by a long short-term memory (LSTM) module rather than the MLP. The hidden layer has 512 neurons as well. (3) **T-ViT** The LSTM module is replaced in this paradigm by a T-ViT. The depth of the transformer module is one, the number of heads is eight, the embedding dimension and number of the hidden layer of the MLP head are 512, and the Q, K, and V dimensions are 64. (4) **ST-ViT** This is our proposed spatial-temporal vision transformer model, which employs a spatial convolutional vision transformer to address feature maps first, as opposed to the T-ViT. The depth and heads of the spatial transformer are the same as those of the temporal transformer; the dimensions of the Q and K are 32, whilst the V is 64.

We use the common threefold cross-evaluation experimental protocol, which divides the dataset into 70 percent (16 videos) for training and 30 percent (8 videos) for testing. The batch size in the training process is 16, Adam is used as the optimizer, and the learning rate is $1 \times e^{-4}$. The metric used is the MAE, which is the same as in other works. The results are shown in Table 3.2. According to the results, the image pair outperforms the single image, and the MAE of the CNN + LSTM model is lower than the Baseline model in all three-fold cross-validation. The T-ViT model is not always competitive when compared to the LSTM model; it simply has a smaller error in the first fold cross-evaluation. Figure 3.11 depicts the overall average performance of the different models.

The above results show that the image pair can improve the performance of the models due to the additional sequential information. To investigate the effect of

Table 3.2 The comparison of several typical models on the BIWI dataset

Videos	Model	Pitch	Yaw	Roll	Avg.
1–8	Baseline	4.135	3.509	4.000	3.881
	LSTM	3.854	3.459	3.929	3.747
	T-ViT	3.831	3.275	3.801	3.636
	ST-ViT	3.795	3.206	3.619	3.540
9–16	Baseline	2.720	2.414	2.535	2.556
	LSTM	2.846	2.154	2.480	2.493
	T-ViT	2.811	2.280	2.628	2.573
	ST-ViT	2.552	2.313	2.568	2.478
17–24	Baseline	3.477	3.465	3.676	3.539
	LSTM	3.163	3.014	3.412	3.196
	T-ViT	3.421	2.961	3.430	3.271
	ST-ViT	3.485	2.955	3.218	3.219

Fig. 3.11 The MAE of
different models

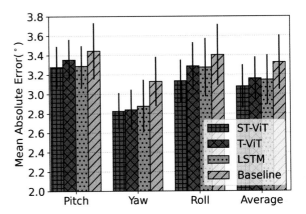

Fig. 3.12 The comparison
of the different lengths of the
sequence input. The *Sn*
means the length of the
sequence *n*

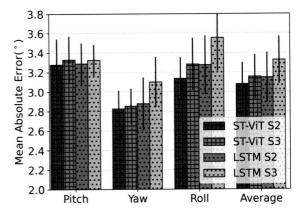

sequence further, we used three consecutive frames as input to train the ST-ViT and
the LSTM, with the results shown in Fig. 3.12. The comparison demonstrates that a
longer sequence causes the model to degenerate, resulting in a higher MAE across all
three axes. The reason for this is that longer sequential information cannot solve the
problem of cross-subject evaluation, and the BIWI's deviation between consecutive
frames is large. The degradation of the LSTM is more severe than that of the ST-
ViT. Even if the input length is the same, the ST-ViT outperforms the LSTM. It
demonstrates that the ST-ViT is more robust than the LSTM when dealing with
sequence data. The ST-ViT can learn the relationship between successive frames and
improve its performance.

To have a comprehensive evaluation, the introduced model is compared with
other state-of-the-art methods. These models use the same training protocol as
well. Because the BIWI dataset includes a depth image, some methods use the
depth information to improve performance [32, 33]. The benefit of the RGB image
combining depth information is also demonstrated in Table 3.3. To improve the
model performance, these methods developed various models and loss functions

Table 3.3 The comparison of the state-of-the-art models on the BIWI dataset

Model	Input	Pitch	Yaw	Roll	Avg.
DeepHeadPose [32]	RGB	5.18	5.67	–	–
DeepHeadPose [32]	RGB + Depth	4.76	5.32	–	–
SSR-Net-MD [14]	RGB	4.35	4.24	4.19	4.26
VGG16 [14]	RGB	4.03	3.91	3.03	3.66
FSA-Caps-Fusion [14]	RGB	4.29	2.89	3.60	3.60
MultiLossResNet50 [15]	RGB	3.39	3.29	3.00	3.23
FDNNet [31]	RGB	3.98	3.00	2.88	3.29
Martin [33]	RGB + Depth	2.50	3.60	2.60	2.90
Baseline	RGB	3.44	3.12	3.40	3.32
LSTM	RGB	3.28	2.87	3.12	3.14
ST-ViT	RGB	3.27	**2.82**	3.12	**3.07**

The bold model name represents the proposed model in this section

from various perspectives. When compared to RGB-based methods, the introduced method achieves the best performance, and it outperforms the depth-based multi-modality method on the yaw axis. The performance of the Baseline and the LSTM also demonstrates the importance of the backbone, providing us with a guideline for future research. The comparison with others demonstrates the efficacy of the introduced method.

The ST-ViT is used to estimate the head pose on the BIWI dataset to evaluate the proposed pipeline. Obviously, the error and variance in the head pose estimation model are unavoidable, and it cannot be used directly for dynamic head tracking. The reasonable approach is to use a filter to smooth the curve. Given that the performance of the head pose model varies depending on the angle range, this section introduces the AKF. To demonstrate, we chose two sequences with different pitch axis angle ranges, and the results are shown in Fig. 3.13. When the KF is applied, the curve is smoothed, and the volatility is decreased. It's worth noting that the ground truth has

Fig. 3.13 The comparison of the standard and adaptive KF during different angle range

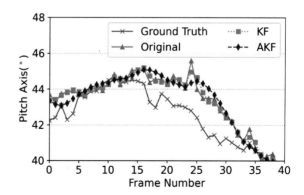

Table 3.4 The comparison of the different filtering methods

Videos	Mean\Std.	Method	Pitch	Yaw	Roll
1–8	Mean	Original	3.795	3.206	3.619
		KF	3.809	3.253	3.631
		AKF	3.803	3.196	3.619
	Std	KF	3.649	3.556	4.342
		AKF	3.632	3.495	4.351
9–16	Mean	Original	2.552	2.313	2.568
		KF	2.618	2.371	2.595
		AKF	2.565	2.329	2.571
	Std	KF	2.473	2.003	3.061
		AKF	2.368	1.924	3.054
17–24	Mean	Original	3.485	2.955	3.218
		KF	3.586	3.121	3.248
		AKF	3.496	3.034	3.213
	Std	KF	3.105	2.595	4.306
		AKF	3.019	2.546	4.304

measurement error and deviation as well. This demonstrates that the filter is necessary and reasonable. The R_k is a constant value that represents the mean error of the head pose estimation model in the standard KF. To improve performance even further, the constant R_k is replaced with the adaptive one mentioned above, and the related parameters are the results of the Gaussian fitting on the dataset. The comparisons show that the curves of the standard Kalman Filter and the filter with adaptive R_k almost coincide at low angles are shown in Table 3.4. The filter with adaptive R_k, on the other hand, performs better at high angle ranges and has a smoother curve. The filtering algorithm strikes a balance between precision and smoothness. The increase in smoothness will inevitably result in a loss of accuracy. The proposed AKF can keep accuracy whilst decreasing variance. This is one of the benefits of the adaptive R_k.

3.3.3   Summary

This section introduces a dynamic head pose tracking system to improve the immersion and interaction of the driving simulator and related application. The introduced method only employs the RGB camera, with no additional hardware or markers. A spatial–temporal vision transformer model is utilized, which uses image pairs as input instead of a single frame to improve the accuracy of dynamic head pose estimation. In addition to the standard transformer, it includes the spatial convolutional vision transformer and the temporal vision transformer, which can improve the model's effectiveness. The results of the extensive experimental comparison show that the proposed method outperforms the state-of-the-art methods. The other challenge in deploying on the head tracking system is that the head pose estimation models still have certain errors that cannot be directly adopted. To address this issue, this section attempts to utilize a filter approach for post-processing raw estimation. By analysing the estimation model's error distribution and user experience, the adaptive KF is adopted, which includes an adaptive observation noise coefficient that can smooth the curve in areas where the estimation model has a high error. Experiments show that the proposed method is reasonable, and it has been implemented in the driving simulator.

The introduced low-cost vision-based solution for head tracking is a framework, which can be further optimized as the head pose estimation algorithm improves. It can also be used in other driver-in-the-loop applications.

3.4 Appearance-Based Eye Gaze Estimation

As previously stated, human interaction is multi-modal which involves various types of activities, where the gaze serving as an important communicative cue that can indicate people's emotional state, attention, and intentions. As a result, it is a critical feature for human–machine interaction. The related studies can be found in various applications and fields, including the driver monitoring system, psychology study, product and web design, rehabilitation, etc. Specifically, there are basically two types of studies for the human gaze: gaze direction estimation [34] and eye fixation tracking [35], as shown in Fig. 3.14. The former needs to estimate the gaze direction, whereas the latter can directly obtain the focused position. Therefore, various sensors and devices are developed to tackle these two tasks. The typical device is the eye-tracking glasses and devices, such as the products of the Tobii company [36], and usually they are expensive. In comparison, this section will still focus on the low-cost vision-based approach leveraging the advanced deep learning approach. The two gaze tasks will be discussed one by one.

Fig. 3.14 The gaze direction estimation (left) and the gaze fixation tracking (right)

3.4.1 Gaze Direction Estimation

The gaze estimation aims to obtain the pitch and yaw angles transformed from a 3d vector, which is similar to the head pose estimation that is to estimate the pitch, yaw, and roll angles. Therefore, there are also two types of approaches in general: geometry-based [37] and appearance-based [38]. The geometry-based approach employs a predefined pattern to detect predefined feature positions, such as pupil position and corner, and then these extracted features are utilized to calculate the gaze direction using geometric relationships. The challenge is that it has stringent requirements for the input image's quality and resolution. The advancement of deep learning allows more researchers to focus on the appearance-based model in a data-driven manner, which enables the gaze direction can be estimated from the low-quality images. To improve performance, researchers proposed various types of CNN-based structures.

The single eye image was used as the input to regression the gaze direction in the classic appearance-based approaches. Some researchers utilized the head pose information to enhance the model performance. However, some studies have shown that the head pose cannot provide the obvious improvement [39]. The reason for this is that the inaccurate head pose estimation, and the different coordinate of the gaze. Some studies proposed some compromise approaches to avoid these issues, such as instead of the head pose by a face image [40], and then they proposed corresponding modules to elicit the network to learn the implicit relationship between the face and the eyes. However, the diversity of the face images could influence the model's robustness about the person's independence. Therefore, the eye image should be separated from the face image, which will be more reasonable. Using the principle of asymmetry between the two eyes, the left and right eyes images were utilized to feed into the model at the same time [41], which aims to discover the hard sample and improve the model performance. They concentrate on asymmetry whilst overlooking the most important consistency feature of the two eyes, which can enhance the model's performance. The preceding discussion is primarily concerned with person-independent methods, where the utilized training and testing samples are captured from different persons. There are also numerous types of studies that focus on the personalized approaches, where the utilized training and testing samples are collected from the same person. The behind assumption is that each people have a personalized bias. Therefore, several label samples from test subjects are needed to calibrate the model [42], which can significantly improve model performance. Some researchers also investigated unsupervised and semi-supervised methods for dealing with this task [43]. This section will go over both the person independent model and the calibration.

1. Methodology
The above section has mentioned that the deep learning is currently shifting from inductive bias models to the fully learnable models leveraging the massive data sets, such as the Transformers [44]. By leveraging the Neural Architecture Search (NAS) technology, several general structures and backbones can be obtained, such as

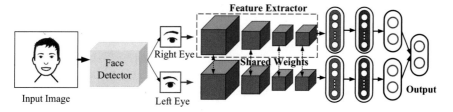

Fig. 3.15 The architecture of the gaze estimation model

the Efficient-Nets [45], which will liberate the researchers from the hyperparameter tuning conundrum.

This section will introduce an appearance-based framework for estimating gaze direction, using a low-cost RGB camera as the input sensor as shown in Fig. 3.15. First, a face detector can be adopted to detect the face landmarks. Following that, the detected bounding box and landmarks are used to propose various regions for the downstream gaze direction estimation model. The advantage of the pre-processing detection is that it can filter out the effects of the background and let the downstream model focus on the specific area to improve the model's robustness. Compared with the face and background, the difference of the eyes between different persons is relatively small, which will benefit the person-independent estimation. Then, a predefined model is utilized to extract the features of the eyes respectively, but the weight of the feature extractor is shared between the two eyes images. Once the features are obtained, they will be tackled by different full connection layers to estimate the gaze direction independently. Finally, the separative estimation will be combined with the final output based on the consistency principle. This kind of design can take advantage of the ensemble learning conception, which employs multiple learning models to achieve better predictive performance than could be obtained from any of the constituent learning models alone.

Humans typically exhibit variability in the appearance of the eyes, the accuracy of the universal model usually has limited performance and tends to present high variance due to the person-dependent biases. To address this issue, some reference-based approaches are proposed. Liu et al. [34] presented a differential CNN model to predict gaze differences between two eye images of the same subject and utilized a set of subject-specific calibration images, and Park et al. [43] proposed a framework that can learn the person-specific gaze with few calibration samples. Lindén et al. [46] adopted a specific model for capturing the personal variations that are considered as in a low-dimensional latent parameter space. To improve the performance of the estimation, all of these approaches require calibration samples. However, reference-based methods can be difficult to implement from a practical standpoint due to the ground truth of the gaze direction is difficult to be obtained.

2. Model Analysis

The MPIIGaze [39] and UT-Multi-view [47] are two commonly used and representative datasets for gaze direction estimation. The MPIIGaze contains 213,659 images collected from 15 participants over a three-month period during normal everyday laptop use. It has a wide range of appearance in the wild and illumination conditions. Only 1500 left and right eye images from each subject are chosen at random to train and test. It provides the corresponding grayscale images that are frontalized based on the head pose. The UT-Multi-view has a total of 50 people (15 female and 35 male) who participated in data collection, and 160 different gaze directions are captured using 8 cameras. The cameras and gaze target plane have been fully calibrated, and all annotations are in the 3D world coordinate system. It also reconstructed 3D shapes of the eye regions. Finally, there are 64,000 real eye images and 1,152,000 synthesized eye images included.

As previously stated, the gaze estimation task has two approaches: reference-free and reference-based models. The reference-based method is similar to the calibrated model in that it requires several calibration dataset reference samples. To compare with them, we calibrate the trained model with varying numbers of reference samples. Some researchers utilize extra information such as the face image or the head pose to improve the model's performance. In our experiments, only the eyes images are utilized. The EfficientNet-b0 is adopted as the backbone to extract the features of the eyes. The results are shown in Table 3.5. The introduced method can achieve the state-of-the-art in both the MPIIGaze and the UT-Multi-view datasets, with the latter outperforming the former.

3.4.2 Gaze Fixation Tracking

In general, gaze fixation tracking necessitates the usage of some specialized devices known as the eye tracker. Most modern eye trackers, such as the Tobii Eye Tracker and SMI REDn, have one or two cameras and one or more infrared light sources to illuminate the facial area to create a corneal reflection, which aims to provide high quality image. The location of the pupil in the camera image is compared to the location of the corneal reflection in the eye tracker to determine the gaze fixation. According to the user's freedom, the gaze fixation tracking systems are classified into three types [60, 61]: (1) Wearable eye tracker, which is worn on the user's head and looks like a pair of glasses, and usually outfitted with a scene camera to infer the user what they are looking at. (2) Mounted eye tracker, which generally utilizes one or more infrared sensors that are fixed in front of the user and allow the user to move freely in a specific field. (3) Head-restricted eye tracker, which constitutes a tower-mounted eye tracker, or a remote eye tracker with a chin rest. It restricts both the chin and the head and films the eyes from above. In comparison, the mounted eye tracker is less intrusive and easier to use. This section describes a similar solution, but only with low-cost cameras.

Data-driven gaze tracking technology has recently gained popularity as a result of the rapid development of deep learning, which promotes the progress of the appearance-based eye tracking study. Zhang et al. [40] proposed a CNN that can suppress or enhance information in different facial regions in a flexible manner

Table 3.5 The comparison of the gaze estimation on the MPIIGaze and the UT-Multi-view dataset

Method		Input		MPIIGaze			UT-multi-view		
		face	Head	Left	Right	Avg.	Left	Right	Avg.
Ref	iTracker [48]	✓	–	5.6	5.6	5.6	–	–	–
	GazeNet [40]	–	✓	5.5	5.5	5.5	4.4	4.4	4.4
	Dilated-Net [49]	✓	–	5.2	5.2	5.2	–	–	–
	MeNet [54]	✓	–	4.9	4.9	4.9	5.5	5.5	5.5
	RT-GENE [57]	✓	–	4.8	4.8	4.8	5.1	5.1	5.1
	RSN [56]	✓	–	4.5	4.5	4.5	–	–	–
	PureGaze [55]	✓	–	4.5	4.5	4.5	–	–	–
	AGENet [50]	✓	–	4.1	4.1	4.1	–	–	–
	BAL-Net [51]	–	–	4.3	4.3	4.3	5.4	5.4	5.4
	LNSMM [53]	–	–	4.8	4.8	4.8	4.8	4.8	4.8
	CrtCLGM [52]	✓	–	–	–	–	5.7	5.7	5.7
	U-Train [58]	–	–	–	–	–	5.5	5.5	5.5
	Our-b0	–	–	3.9	4.0	3.95	3.0	3.0	3.0
nRef	DEANet [59]	–	✓	4.4	4.4	4.4	3.6	3.6	3.6
	Diff-NN [34]	–	–	4.7	4.6	4.65	4.2	4.1	4.15
	Diff-VGG [34]	–	–	3.9	3.7	3.8	3.9	3.7	3.8
	Our-b0(5)	–	–	3.2	3.3	3.25	2.8	2.8	2.8
	Our-b0(10)	–	–	3.2	3.2	3.2	2.6	2.6	2.6
	Our-b0(10)	–	–	3.0	3.0	3.0	2.4	2.4	2.4

without considering the position of the face. TabletGaze [62] provided an unconstrained gaze dataset of tablet users who differed in race, gender, and glasses. A multi-level HoG feature is proposed, which is combined with a random forest regressor to tackle the task. Li et al. [63] utilized an eye tracker to collect the gaze position whilst training a gaze estimation model to achieve the data-driven estimation. iTracker [64] collected the first large-scale eye tracking dataset, which included data from over 1450 people and nearly 2.5 million frames. Using the collected dataset, they trained a CNN that outperformed previous approaches in terms of error reduction whilst running in real time. The introduced method of this section basically follows its study. Hu et al. [25] leveraged a dual-view camera that combined the saliency map and semantic information from a scene, whereas TurkerGaze [65] regressed the position of the eye using the saliency map and support vector regression (SVR). Simultaneously, Yang et al. [66] also presented a dual-camera-based calibrated gaze mapping system that established the correspondence relation using the orthogonal least squares algorithm. The existing studies show that more researchers pay attention to the appearance-based approach leveraging the data-driven manner beside the specific devices and sensors.

1. Methodology

The main goal of this section is to introduce a real-time gaze-tracking system using only a low-cost camera, where the computer screen is serving as the application platform. A data-driven approach utilizing a CNN model should be the reasonable solution. The overall architecture of the introduced method is depicted in Fig. 3.16. The webcam is utilized to capture a frontal image of the user whilst estimating the gaze fixation position relative to the camera. A face detection module is adopted to detect the bounding box and keypoints of the face from the captured image. The raw image is split into four branches with various kinds of feature maps after preprocessing: right eye map, left eye map, face map, and face grid map. The face and eye map are fed into two different CNN-based feature extractors, where the left eye and right eye maps share the same extractor. Then the extracted feature maps are reshaped into one-dimension vectors. The face grid map is directly reshaped to a one-dimension vector. These vectors will be concatenated and fed into the output module with full connection layers to estimate the fixation position. A calibration step is design to fine-tune and optimize the trained model's performance.

The most important cues for gaze tracking are head pose and eye gaze. To allow the model to focus on them, a face detector can be utilized to extract the face and eyes area instead of using the raw image as input map. The current face detection technology is well-developed and has been used in a number of successful commercial applications. The MTCNN [18] can be adopted in the face detection module, which employs a carefully designed cascaded architecture to detect the human face and landmarks in a coarse-to-fine manner. Its accuracy outperforms the face detection benchmarks in the open datasets, as well as the face alignment benchmarks whilst maintaining

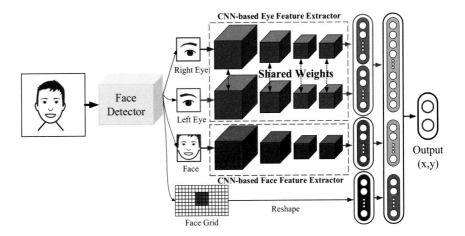

Fig. 3.16 The architecture of the gaze fixation tracking approach

real-time performance. Leveraging the face detector, the face and eye areas can be cropped, which also benefits to improve the robustness of the model in tackling various types of back-grounds. Due to the gaze direction being coupled with the position and orientation of the head, the user's relative position to the camera is also important and should be taken into account. As a result, the face grid is designed to represent the face's relative position. The raw image is divided into several grids, with the corresponding grids of the face area set to 1 and the others set to 0. The size of the face area can indicate the distance of the head. It is then reshaped into a one-dimensional vector to integrated with others.

The introduced gaze-tracking system is basically utilized to estimate the fixation position in a computer screen. Therefore, we can require the person to stare at a specific dot display on the screen, whilst capturing the frontal image of the person. During the dataset collection, various dots are randomly displayed on the screen, and each time display should have a reasonable interval considering the human reaction time, which ensures that the captured image and its ground truth correspond correctly. The training set and testing set should be person-independent, which means the training subjects are different from the testing ones. This principle is very important to fairly evaluate the utilized model. However, given the variety of subject eyes and habits, the calibration step is introduced to improve the model performance, which is inspired by the work of [65] as shown in Fig. 3.17. There were 13 fixed position dots that are utilized to fine-tune the model in order to calibrate a new subject.

2. Model Analysis

The GazeCapture [64] is the first large-scale dataset for gaze tracking, which collected data from over 1450 people and nearly 2.5 million frames. Based on the collected dataset, they train a convolutional neural network for eye tracking called iTracker, which achieves a significant reduction in error over previous approaches whilst running in real time (10–15 fps) on a modern mobile device. However, the Gaze-Capture is collected by the smartphone, which means that it is not suitable for the estimating the gaze fixation on the computer screen. It takes a long time to collect a new dataset with millions of samples. That's when transfer learning inspired us to find a new solution, where we can fine-tune the trained iTracker model using a small dataset for the computer screen.

Fig. 3.17 The layout of the dot display for the calibration

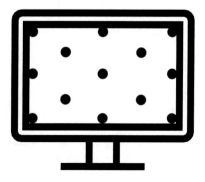

Table 3.6 The comparison with the state-of-the-art methods

	Model	Mean error (cm)	Methodology
Long distance	**Our, no cali**	3.8	Without calibration
	Our, cali	3.2	With calibration
	Li [63]	4.6	Full face + CNN
	TurkerGaze [65]	4.8	Saliency map + SVR
	Zhang [40]	4.2	Full face + CNN
	EyeNet [67]	4.6	Sequential frames
	Lian [68]	4.7	Multi-task CNN
	LNSMM [53]	3.9	Multi-task with multiple datasets
	Gudi [69]	4.2	Hybrid geometric regression
Short distance	TabletGaze [62]	3.2	HOG + RF for tablet
	iTracker [64]	2.6	CNN for smartphone

The bold model name represents the proposed model in this section

To evaluate the gaze-tracking model, a dataset was collected from 13 subjects (2 females and 11 males, 10 with glasses and 3 without glasses) using the experimental platform depicted in the above section. A script was created that displayed the dot on the screen at random. A response time of 1000 ms was provided for each frame to allow the user to follow the randomly displayed dots. To alleviate user fatigue, the colour of the dot was also changed at random. Each subject contributed to eight data groups, with each group containing 100 frames. In the end, our data set contained 10,400 samples. In addition, 13 fixed calibration frames are collected for each subject. To validate the performance and robustness of the proposed method, the data from 6 subjects was used as the test set and the data from the remaining 7 subjects as the training set.

Leveraging the collected dataset, the introduced model's feature extractor is instead and initialized by the corresponding modules of the pre-trained iTracker model, and then the model is trained using the training samples. The 13 fixed calibration frames are utilized to fine-tune the trained model. The experimental results can be found in Table 3.6, which demonstrates that the calibration can significantly improve the model performance. The introduced model can outperform other state-of-the-art methods for long-distance gaze tracking. It still can compete with the short distance ones which are utilized for the smartphone or tablet.

3.5 Summary

This chapter has introduced the facial-related explicit activities using the low-cost camera, including head pose estimation, head pose tracking, gaze direction estimation, and gaze fixation tracking. These activities are important cues that can indicate human attention and intention, which are the key technique to construct the harmonious human–machine system. The corresponding available datasets are introduced for the related researcher reference. The main challenge of the head pose and gaze tasks is the accurate dataset, and its difficulty is exacerbated by the diversity of human beings. Some researchers utilized the synthesize technology to generate the corresponding ground truth of the samples, this kind of approach will inevitably reduce the realistic and naturalistic of the samples. Leveraging the advanced deep learning approach, the existing studies have achieved outstanding performance; however, they also reached the limit. In the future, the researchers should pay more attention to the dataset collection, especially the multi-modal corpus that includes the head pose and gaze simultaneously. The accurate and large dataset can promote the studies to a higher level.

References

1. Pantic M, Rothkrantz LJM (2000) Automatic analysis of facial expressions: the state of the art. IEEE Trans Pattern Anal Mach Intell 22(12):1424–1445
2. Picard RW (2000) Affective computing. MIT Press (2000)
3. Zyner A, Worrall S, Nebot E (2019) Naturalistic driver intention and path prediction using recurrent neural networks. IEEE Trans Intell Transp Syst 21(4):1584–1594
4. Hu Z, Xing Y, Lv C, Hang P, Liu J (2021) Deep convolutional neural network-based bernoulli heatmap for head pose estimation. Neurocomputing 436:198–209
5. Hu Z, Zhang Y, Xing Y, Zhao Y, Cao D, Lv C (2022) Toward human-centered automated driving: A novel spatiotemporal vision transformer-enabled head tracker. IEEE Veh Technol Mag 2–9
6. Zhang X, Sugano Y, Fritz M, Bulling A (2015) Appearance-based gaze estimation in the wild. In: Proceedings of the IEEE conference on computer vision and pattern recognition, pp 4511–4520
7. Luo C, Zhang J, Yu J, Chen CW, Wang S (2019) Real-time head pose estimation and face modeling from a depth image. IEEE Trans Multimedia 21(10):2473–2481
8. Borghi G, Fabbri M, Vezzani R, Calderara S, Cucchiara R (2018) Face-from-depth for head pose estimation on depth images. IEEE Trans Pattern Anal Mach Intell 42(3):596–609
9. Yu Y, Mora KAF, Odobez J-M (2018) Headfusion: 360 head pose tracking combining 3d morphable model and 3d reconstruction. IEEE Trans Pattern Anal Mach Intell 40(11):2653–2667
10. Yuan H, Li M, Hou J, Xiao J (2020) Single image-based head pose estimation with spherical parametrization and 3d morphing. Pattern Recogn 103:107316
11. Barros JMD, Mirbach B, Garcia F, Varanasi K, Stricker D (2018) Fusion of keypoint tracking and facial landmark detection for real-time head pose estimation. In: 2018 IEEE winter conference on applications of computer vision (WACV). IEEE, pp 2028–2037
12. Gou C, Wu Y, Wang F-Y, Ji Q (2017) Coupled cascade regression for simultaneous facial landmark detection and head pose estimation. In: 2017 IEEE international conference on image processing (ICIP). IEEE, pp 2906–2910
13. Hsu H-W, Wu T-Y, Wan S, Wong WH, Lee C-Y (2018) Quatnet: Quaternion-based head pose estimation with multiregression loss. IEEE Trans Multimedia 21(4):1035–1046
14. Yang T-Y, Chen Y-T, Lin Y-Y, Chuang Y-Y (2019) Fsa-net: learning fine-grained structure aggregation for head pose estimation from a single image. In: Proceedings of the IEEE/CVF conference on computer vision and pattern recognition, pp 1087–1096

15. Ruiz N, Chong E, Rehg JM (2018) Fine-grained head pose estimation without keypoints. In: Proceedings of the IEEE conference on computer vision and pattern recognition workshops, pp 2074–2083
16. Lathuilière S, Juge R, Mesejo P, Munoz-Salinas R, Horaud R (2017) Deep mixture of linear inverse regressions applied to head-pose estimation. In: Proceedings of the IEEE conference on computer vision and pattern recognition, pp 4817–4825
17. Huang B, Chen R, Xu W, Zhou Q (2020) Improving head pose estimation using two-stage ensembles with top-k regression. Image Vis Comput 93:103827
18. Sun K, Xiao B, Liu D, Wang J (2019) Deep high-resolution representation learning for human pose estimation. In: Proceedings of the IEEE/CVF conference on computer vision and pattern recognition, pp 5693–5703
19. Lin M, Chen Q, Yan S (2013) Network in network. arXiv:1312.4400
20. Luo W, Li Y, Urtasun R, Zemel R (2016) Understanding the effective receptive field in deep convolutional neural networks. In: Advances in neural information processing systems, vol 29
21. Zhang Y, Li K, Li K, Wang L, Zhong B, Fu Y (2018) Image super-resolution using very deep residual channel attention networks. In: Proceedings of the European conference on computer vision (ECCV), pp 286–301
22. Fanelli G, Dantone M, Gall J, Fossati A, Van Gool L (2013) Random forests for real time 3d face analysis. Int J Comput Vision 101(3):437–458
23. Zhu X, Lei Z, Liu X, Shi H, Li SZ (2016) Face alignment across large poses: a 3d solution. In: Proceedings of the IEEE conference on computer vision and pattern recognition, pp 146–155
24. Shah S, Dey D, Lovett C, Kapoor A (2018) Airsim: high-fidelity visual and physical simulation for autonomous vehicles. In: Field and service robotics. Springer, pp 621–635
25. Hu Z, Lv C, Hang P, Huang C, Xing Y (2021) Data-driven estimation of driver attention using calibration-free eye gaze and scene features. IEEE Trans Industr Electron 69(2):1800–1808
26. Sim N, Gavriel C, Abbott WW, Faisal AA (2013) The head mouse-head gaze estimation "in-the-wild" with low-cost inertial sensors for BMI use. In: 2013 6th International IEEE/EMBS conference on neural engineering (NER). IEEE, pp 735–738
27. Kang CH, Park CG, Song JW (2016) An adaptive complementary kalman filter using fuzzy logic for a hybrid head tracker system. IEEE Trans Instrum Meas 65(9):2163–2173
28. Ng AK, Chan LK, Lau HY (2017) A low-cost lighthouse-based virtual reality head tracking system. In: 2017 International conference on 3D immersion (IC3D). IEEE, pp 1–5
29. Valle R, Buenaposada JM, Baumela L (2020) Multi-task head pose estimation in-the-wild. IEEE Trans Pattern Anal Mach Intell 43(8):2874–2881
30. Graham B, El-Nouby A, Touvron H, Stock P, Joulin A, Jégou H, Douze M (2021) Levit: a vision transformer in convnet's clothing for faster inference. In: Proceedings of the IEEE/CVF international conference on computer vision, pp 12259–12269
31. Zhang H, Wang M, Liu Y, Yuan Y (2020) FDN: feature decoupling network for head pose estimation. In: Proceedings of the AAAI conference on artificial intelligence, vol 34, pp 12789–12796
32. Mukherjee SS, Robertson NM (2015) Deep head pose: Gaze-direction estimation in multimodal video. IEEE Trans Multimedia 17(11):2094–2107
33. Martin M, Van De Camp F, Stiefelhagen R (2014) Real time head model creation and head pose estimation on consumer depth cameras. In: 2014 2nd international conference on 3D vision, vol 1. IEEE, pp 641–648
34. Liu G, Yu Y, Mora KAF, Odobez J-M (2019) A differential approach for gaze estimation. IEEE Trans Pattern Anal Mach Intell 43(3):1092–1099
35. Kar A, Corcoran P (2019) Gazevisual: A practical software tool and web application for performance evaluation of eye tracking systems. IEEE Trans Consum Electron 65(3):293–302
36. Niehorster DC, Hessels RS, Benjamins JS (2020) Glassesviewer: Open-source software for viewing and analyzing data from the Tobii pro glasses 2 eye tracker. Behav Res Methods 52(3):1244–1253
37. Albiero V, Chen X, Yin X, Pang G, Hassner T (2021) img2pose: face alignment and detection via 6dof, face pose estimation. In: Proceedings of the IEEE/CVF conference on computer vision and pattern recognition, pp 7617–7627

38. Cheng Y, Lu F, Zhang X (2018) Appearance-based gaze estimation via evaluation-guided asymmetric regression. In: Proceedings of the European conference on computer vision (ECCV), pp 100–115
39. Zhang X, Sugano Y, Fritz M, Bulling A (2017) Mpiigaze: real-world dataset and deep appearance-based gaze estimation. IEEE Trans Pattern Anal Mach Intell 41(1):162–175
40. Zhang X, Sugano Y, Fritz M, Bulling A (2017) It's written all over your face: Full-face appearance-based gaze estimation. In: Proceedings of the IEEE conference on computer vision and pattern recognition workshops, pp 51–60
41. Cheng Y, Zhang X, Lu F, Sato Y (2020) Gaze estimation by exploring two-eye asymmetry. IEEE Trans Image Process 29:5259–5272
42. He J, Pham K, Valliappan N, Xu P, Roberts C, Lagun D, Navalpakkam V (2019) On-device few-shot personalization for real-time gaze estimation. In: Proceedings of the IEEE/CVF international conference on computer vision workshops, pp 0–0
43. Park S, Mello SD, Molchanov P, Iqbal U, Hilliges O, Kautz J (2019) Few-shot adaptive gaze estimation. In: Proceedings of the IEEE/CVF international conference on computer vision, pp 9368–9377
44. Guo Y, Zheng Y, Tan M, Chen Q, Li Z, Chen J, Zhao P, Huang J (2021) Towards accurate and compact architectures via neural architecture transformer. IEEE Trans Pattern Anal Mach Intell
45. Tan M, Le Q (2019) Efficientnet: rethinking model scaling for convolutional neural networks. In: International conference on machine learning. PMLR, pp 6105–6114
46. Lindén E, Sjostrand J, Proutiere A (2019) Learning to personalize in appearance-based gaze tracking. In: Proceedings of the IEEE/CVF international conference on computer vision workshops, pp 0–0
47. Sugano Y, Matsushita Y, Sato Y (2014) Learning-by-synthesis for appearance-based 3d gaze estimation. In: Proceedings of the IEEE conference on computer vision and pattern recognition, pp 1821–1828
48. Sun B, Ma Q, Cao Z, Liu Y (2019) iTracker: towards sustained self-tracking in dynamic feature environment with smartphones. In: 2019 16th Annual IEEE international conference on sensing, communication, and networking (SECON). IEEE, pp 1–9
49. Chen Z, Shi BE (2018) Appearance-based gaze estimation using dilated-convolutions. In: Asian conference on computer vision. Springer, pp 309–324
50. Biswas P et al (2021) Appearance-based gaze estimation using attention and difference mechanism. In: Proceedings of the IEEE/CVF conference on computer vision and pattern recognition, pp 3143–3152
51. Wang K, Zhao R, Su H, Ji Q (2019) Generalizing eye tracking with Bayesian adversarial learning. In: Proceedings of the IEEE/CVF conference on computer vision and pattern recognition, pp 11907–11916
52. Yu Y, Liu G, Odobez J-M (2018) Deep multitask gaze estimation with a constrained landmark-gaze model. In: Proceedings of the European conference on computer vision (ECCV) workshops, pp 0–0
53. Huang Y, Chen B, Qu D (2021) LNSMM: Eye gaze estimation with local network share multiview multitask. arXiv:2101.07116
54. Xiong Y, Kim HJ, Singh V (2019) Mixed effects neural networks (menets) with applications to gaze estimation. In: Proceedings of the IEEE/CVF conference on computer vision and pattern recognition, pp 7743–7752
55. Cheng Y, Bao Y, Lu F (2021) PureGaze: purifying gaze feature for generalizable gaze estimation. arXiv:2103.13173
56. Zhang X, Sugano Y, Bulling A, Hilliges O (2020) Learning-based region selection for end-to-end gaze estimation. In: BMVC (2020)
57. Fischer T, Chang HJ, Demiris Y (2018) Rt-gene: Real-time eye gaze estimation in natural environments. In: Proceedings of the European conference on computer vision (ECCV), pp 334–352

58. Dubey N, Ghosh S, Dhall A (2019) Unsupervised learning of eye gaze representation from the web. In: 2019 International joint conference on neural networks (IJCNN). IEEE, pp 1–7
59. Gu S, Wang L, He L, He X, Wang J (2021) Gaze estimation via a differential eyes appearances network with a reference grid. Engineering 7(6):777–786
60. Valtakari NV, Hooge IT, Viktorsson C, Nyström P, Falck-Ytter T, Hessels RS (2021) Eye tracking in human interaction: possibilities and limitations. Behav Res Methods 53(4):1592–1608
61. Su D, Li Y-F, Chen H (2019) Cross-validated locally polynomial modeling for 2-d/3-d gaze tracking with head-worn devices. IEEE Trans Industr Inf 16(1):510–521
62. Huang Q, Veeraraghavan A, Sabharwal A (2017) Tabletgaze: dataset and analysis for unconstrained appearance-based gaze estimation in mobile tablets. Mach Vis Appl 28(5):445–461
63. Li W, Dong Q, Jia H, Zhao S, Wang Y, Xie L, Pan Q, Duan F, Liu T (2019) Training a camera to perform long-distance eye tracking by another eye-tracker. IEEE Access 7:155313–155324
64. Krafka K, Khosla A, Kellnhofer P, Kannan H, Bhandarkar S, Matusik W, Torralba A (2016) Eye tracking for everyone. In: Proceedings of the IEEE conference on computer vision and pattern recognition, pp 2176–2184
65. Xu P, Ehinger KA, Zhang Y, Finkelstein A, Kulkarni SR, Xiao J (2015) Turkergaze: crowdsourcing saliency with webcam based eye tracking. arXiv:1504.06755
66. Yang L, Dong K, Dmitruk AJ, Brighton J, Zhao Y (2019) A dual-cameras-based driver gaze mapping system with an application on non-driving activities monitoring. IEEE Trans Intell Transp Syst 21(10):4318–4327
67. Park S, Aksan E, Zhang X, Hilliges O (2020) Towards end-to-end video-based eye-tracking. In: European conference on computer vision. Springer, pp 747–763
68. Lian D, Zhang Z, Luo W, Hu L, Wu M, Li Z, Yu J, Gao S (2019) RGBD based gaze estimation via multi-task CNN. In: Proceedings of the AAAI conference on artificial intelligence, vol 33, pp 2488–2495
69. Gudi A, Li X, Gemert JV (2020) Efficiency in real-time webcam gaze tracking. In: European conference on computer vision. Springer, pp 529–543

Chapter 4
Vision-Based Body Activity Recognition

Abstract The chapter systematically sorts out the human body-related activity recognition tasks based on the visual sensors, including body pose estimation, action recognition, and body reconstruction. The corresponding state-of-the-art approaches are summarized and introduced. As an important interaction cue, human body activity has broad application scenarios. Therefore, it has attracted considerable attention to improving the accuracy, efficiency, and robustness of the recognition and address the challenges of its diversity and complexity. Basically, there are two kinds of approaches for it: model-based and data-driven. It can clearly see that the data-driven implicit modelling will potentially unify these two approaches, which is a promising direction.

4.1 Introduction

Human body activity recognition systems are required for a variety of applications ranging from health care and assistive technologies to manufacturing and gaming. The use of multi-modal setups involving on-body, object-placed, or ambient sensors is now possible thanks to advances in sensing technology. From the standpoint of machine learning, activity recognition is a difficult problem because it typically deals with high-dimensional, multi-modal streams of data with high variability. Furthermore, real-world deployments must detect when no relevant action is taken. As a result, robust methods for dealing with issues ranging from feature selection and classification to decision fusion and fault-tolerance are required [1].

Usually, the wearable sensors can provide a more robust perception. However, it necessitates the user's physical interaction with the acquisition machine or device. As a result, this approach is increasingly being abandoned because physical contact requires specific skills and sophisticated equipment, which are only available to experienced users. Therefore, wearable sensors must be simple, efficient, and of sufficient size, as well as benefit from user acceptability and willingness to perform continuous monitoring tasks. Amongst the current studies of the body activity, the vision-based should be distinguished, which attempts to simplify the task of human–computer interaction by allowing humans to communicate in a natural and intuitive manner. Intuitively, because vision-based approach only utilizes captured images or recorded video sequences, they may have an advantage over alternative approaches in gaining societal trust.

On the other hand, the vision-based approach more relies on the advancement of the utilized algorithm due to the high diversity, high-dimensional, and high sensitivity of the visual data. The development of deep learning technology promotes its progress. In the computer vision community, body activity recognition has emerged as a hot research topic. It works on many important applications, including human–computer interaction (HCI), virtual reality, security, video surveillance, and home monitoring. As a result, the variety of activity recognition methods is directly related to the application domain in which they are implemented.

The existing body activity-related tasks can be classified into three categories: body pose estimation, body action recognition, and body reconstruction as shown in Fig. 4.1. The body pose estimation is a popular topic and has attracted numerous attentions, which can be split into single person pose estimation and multiple persons pose estimation, whilst the pose includes the 2D pose and 3D pose. For the multiple persons, the utilized approaches basically followed two kinds of manners: top-down and bottom-up. The top-down approach firstly detects the various people of the input, and then the pose of these people is estimated one by one. The bottom-up method usually detects all body keypoints in the in-put image, these keypoints are divided into different people leveraging some planning algorithms. Furthermore, the pose estimation method can be classified into two kinds of approaches: model-based and data-driven, which are similar to the hand pose estimation and head pose

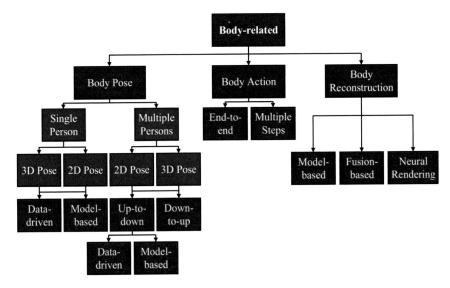

Fig. 4.1 Taxonomy of the vision-based body activity recognition

estimation. The body action recognition can also leverage the estimated pose skeleton to recognize the specific action, which will reduce the complexity of the task. Due to the powerful learning ability of deep learning, many end-to-end models are proposed to directly recognize the action. For the body reconstruction, there are basically three types of methodology. The first is the model-based, which morphs a pre-defined model to fit the input image. The second is to consider it as an optimization task to fuse the input sequential images which include the various views of the body. The last one is the cutting-edge concept, which leverages a trained neural network to render the body model, the trained network has included the implicit mapping relationship between the 2d map and the 3d model voxel. These topics will be described in the following sections.

4.2   Vision-Based Body Pose Estimation

The body pose estimation is similar to the hand pose, which aims to obtain the skeleton keypoints of the body that can indicate the human pose as shown in Fig. 4.3. According to the number of the person in the input image, the pose estimation task can be split into single-person estimation and multi-person estimation. The single-person estimation can be considered as a specific situation of the multi-person one, as well as the utilized methodology. Therefore, this section will focus on the multi-person estimation.

From the pipeline of the utilized method, the multi-person estimation includes two kinds of methods: top-down and bottom-up, as shown in Fig. 4.2. The previous section has explained the difference between them. The former one is to detect the different humans firstly, and then it is transformed into the single-person estimation task. The latter one is to estimate all skeleton keypoints, and then connect the keypoints that belong to the same person. Furthermore, the model-based estimation method is

Fig. 4.2 Illustrations of the top-down and the bottom-up approach for pose estimation

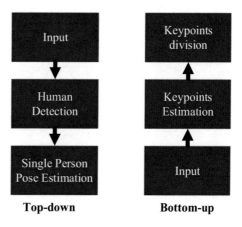

Fig. 4.3 Human body pose
estimation

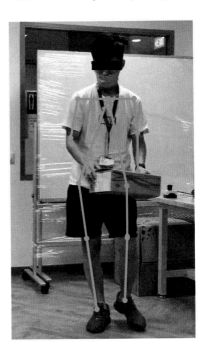

basically utilized in the top-down approach because it needs to know each person's
area. The bottom-up approach primarily utilizes the data-driven method.

4.2.1 Top-Down Methods for Pose Estimation

The top-down approach is more in line with the general logic of human beings, where
the human is firstly detected and then each person's pose is estimated based on the
specific cropped area. Therefore, it relies on two main modules. The first is the human
detection model. In the traditional pattern recognition studies, some specific feature
descriptors and methods are developed for human detection, the represented one is
the HOG descriptor which counts occurrences of gradient orientation in localized
portions of the images, and it is thus particularly suited for human detection [2].
Currently, deep learning has a predominant role in object detection, where human is a
typical object that can be detected. Therefore, the current human detection basically
leverages the cutting-edge object detection model, which can provide the human
positions in images.

Once the human area is cropped, the single human pose estimation method can
be activated. The mainstream method is to adopt the CNN-based models. At first,
the model usually directly regresses the keypoint positions by leveraging the full
connection layer to tackle the extracted feature maps. However, the researchers found
that the directly regression is an extremely non-linear process; the loss function's

weight constraint will be relatively weak, and the spatial information of the feature map will be lost. As a result, the Gaussian heatmap approach is the primary output of the human pose estimation, where each joint has a corresponding heatmap. The Bernoulli heatmap approach for the head pose, which is not the same as the body pose, was briefly discussed in the previous chapter. The same characteristic is that both heatmaps can indicate the interest region by activating the corresponding area in the heatmap. The difference is that the head bounding box can be detected and cropped, the direct regression can be used instead of the heatmap at this time. However, it is difficult to crop all of the human body's joint areas, resulting in the Gaussian heatmap playing a dominant role in human pose estimation at the moment. The main advantage of the heatmap is that it can leverage the convolutional layer's spatial perception capability to form a full convolutional network without requiring the full connection layer, which is benefit to the converging and the robustness of the model.

The existing studies of the human pose estimation mainly focus on the structure design of the CNN-based model. As we know, the success of CNN is attributed to the multi-levels of features and the multi-scales of perception. The above chapters have also discussed the significant performance of the multi-scale network. Similar, the current state-of-the-art model for human pose estimation is the deep high-resolution representation network (HRNet) [3]. The majority of existing CNN-based models recover high-resolution representations from low-resolution representations generated by a high-to-low resolution network. Rather, the HRNet keeps high-resolution representations throughout the process, which begins with a high-resolution subnetwork, then adds high-to-low resolution subnetworks one by one to form more stages, and then connects the multi-resolution subnetworks in parallel. It performs repeated multi-scale fusions so that each of the high-to-low resolution representations repeatedly receives information from other parallel representations, resulting in rich high-resolution representations, as shown in Fig. 4.4. Therefore, the predicted keypoint heatmap may be more accurate and precise in terms of spatial precision (Fig. 4.5).

The above mainly focus on the 2D pose estimation leveraging the data-driven manner. In comparison, the 3d human pose estimation is a more challenging task, which can provide more information, resulting in promising applications in various tasks, including motion capture, action understanding, human–robot interaction, surveillance, etc. We also can utilize the direct regression methods, which frequently make use of a multi-sensor equipped environment, such as multi-view cameras [4, 5], depth images [6, 7], and video streams [8, 9]. For the unconstrained single 2d image, the more robust method is to leverage the 2d pose as an intermediate output to form a cascade pipeline, this kind of approach can take advantage of the advancement of 2D image understanding, which has been made possible by the undeniable impact of deep learning. Even in the presence of occlusion, cutting-edge methods perform surprisingly well at 2D pose estimation. How to predict depth values for the estimated 2D joints is the final challenge. In computer vision, inferring 3D structure from 2D correspondences is a well-studied problem that is frequently addressed in multi-view settings as structure from motion. The relevant cues in the context of monocular human pose estimation appear to be semantic rather than geometric. Based on high-level knowledge derived from anthropometric, kinematic, and dynamic constraints,

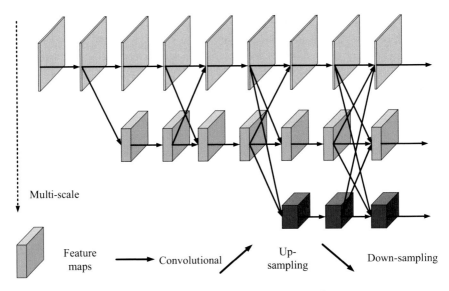

Fig. 4.4 The multi-scale structure keeping high-resolution representation

Fig. 4.5 The pipeline of the data-driven 3d human pose estimation

one can estimate 3D postures from a 2D skeleton. This is traditionally treated as a constrained optimization problem with the goal of minimizing the 2D reprojection error of an unknown 3D pose and unknown camera [10–12]. The optimization problem is frequently constrained by kinematic constraints [13, 14], and 3D poses are sometimes assumed to exist in a low-dimensional subspace to better condition the optimization. Such optimization-based approaches may be sensitive to initialization and local minima, and they frequently necessitate the use of expensive constrained solvers. Some studies proposed a data-driven matching approach to alleviate this issue by leveraging a pre-defined 3d pose library, which results in a quick and accurate 3D solution when combined with a simple closed-form warping algorithm [15] (Fig. 4.6).

Except the data-driven approach, there is another model-based method, which utilizes a deformable model to fit the image or pose joints. The typical and popular model is called Skinned Multi-Person Linear (SMPL) model [16], which is a realistic 3D model of the human body that is based on skinning and blend shapes and is learned from thousands of 3D body scans. The parameters of the model are learned from data including the rest pose template, blend weights, pose-dependent blend shapes, identity-dependent blend shapes, and a regressor from vertices to joint locations. This

Fig. 4.6 The model-based
human pose estimation

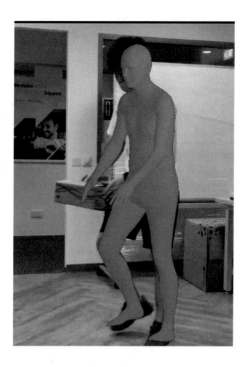

simple formulation enables training the entire model from a relatively large number
of aligned 3D meshes of different people in different poses. Then the 3D deformable
model can be fitted with the image key cues, such as the joints, by minimizing an
objective function that penalizes the error between the projected 3D model joints and
detected 2D joints. We can robustly fit SMPL to very little data because it captures
correlations in human shape across the population [17]. The key problem of this kind
of method is the objective function design, which can significantly affect the final
fitting performance. Except for the joints, the silhouettes or face pose can also be
involved to optimize the fitting.

4.2.2 Bottom-Up Methods for Pose Estimation

Aside from the top-to-down approach for human pose estimation, another common
method is the bottom-up approach, which first obtains the different types of joints of
various people in the input image, then determines which joints belong to the same
person to achieve multi-person pose estimation. The top-down approaches directly
leverage existing techniques for single-person pose estimation but suffer from some
disadvantages: if the person detector fails—as it frequently does when people are in
close proximity—there is no way to recover. Furthermore, the computational cost
of these top-down approaches increases with the number of people. The bottom-up

approaches, on the other hand, are appealing because they the potential to decouple runtime complexity from the number of people in the image, and do not directly use global contextual cues from other body parts and people.

The main challenge of the bottom-up approach is the final parsing process for determining the detected joints of various people. Pishchulin et al. [18], for example, proposed a bottom-up approach that jointly labelled part detection candidates and associated them with individual people. The integer linear programming problem over a fully connected graph, on the other hand, is an NP-hard problem with an average processing time of hours. Insafutdinov et al. [19] improved on [20] by using stronger part detectors and image-dependent pairwise scores, but the method still takes several minutes per image and has a limit on the number of part proposals. The pairwise representations used in [19] are difficult to regress precisely, necessitating a separate logistic regression. The milestone and representative work is the OpenPose [21], which presents an efficient method for multi-person pose estimation with state-of-the-art accuracy. It proposes a novel bottom-up representation of association scores using Part Affinity Fields, which are a collection of 2D vector fields that encode the location and orientation of limbs across the image domain. Leveraging these bottom-up representations of detection and association at the same time encodes global context sufficiently well, which allows a greedy parse to produce high-quality results at a fraction of the computational cost.

The overall pipeline of the OpenPose can be found in Fig. 4.7, which takes a colour image as input and produces the 2D locations of anatomical keypoints for each person in the image as output. To begin, a feedforward network predicts a set of 2D confidence maps S of body part locations as well as a set of 2D vector fields L of part affinities, which encode the degree of association between parts. Finally, greedy inference is used to parse the confidence maps and affinity fields to produce the 2D keypoints for all people in the image. It has demonstrated that it can maintain efficiency even as the number of people in the image increases on some open benchmarks.

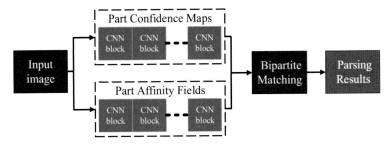

Fig. 4.7 Illustration of the overall pipeline of the OpenPose

4.2.3 Common Datasets

For the 2D human pose estimation, there are several open datasets, including: LSP [20], FLIC [22], MPII [23], MS COCO [24], and PoseTrack [25]. The commonly used is the MPII and the COCO dataset, where the former includes the single and multi-person pose samples, and the latter mainly includes the multi-person samples. The PoseTrack is mainly used for the evaluation of the pose tracking methods.

The MPII Human Pose dataset is a cutting-edge benchmark for evaluating articulated human pose estimation. The dataset contains approximately 25 K images of over 40 K people with annotated body joints. The images were collected in a systematic manner using an established taxonomy of everyday human activities. The dataset covers 410 human activities in total, and each image is labelled with an activity label. Each image was extracted from a YouTube video and was accompanied by unannotated frames preceding and following it. Furthermore, for the test set, it obtained more detailed annotations such as body part occlusions and 3D torso and head orientations.

The MS COCO (Microsoft Common Objects in Context) is a large-scale dataset for object detection, segmentation, key-point detection, and captioning. There are 328K images in the dataset. DensePose annotations have been applied to over 39,000 images and 56,000 person instances, and each labelled person is annotated with an instance id and a mapping between image pixels belonging to that person body and a template 3D model. Only the annotations for training and validation images are made public.

For the 3D human pose estimation, the typical datasets include: Human3.6M [26], HumanEva [27], Total Capture [28], JTA Dataset [29], MPI-INF-3DHP [30], SURREAL [31], UP-3D [32], and DensePose COCO [33]. In comparison, the 3D pose is far more complex than the 2D in the data processing stage. In terms of datasets and models, 2D human posture recognition is more mature than 3D. Although there are many outdoor and natural datasets for 2D models, almost all 3D datasets are indoor or synchronized. The complexity of 3D labelling and recognition necessitates the use of a large number of sensors and cameras to collect data.

4.3 Vision-Based Action Recognition

Vision-based actions in videos can be subdivided into two tasks: recognition and prediction. The action recognition is used to infer human actions (present state) based on complete action executions, whilst action prediction is used to predict human actions (future state) based on incomplete action executions. These two tasks have recently become particularly popular topics due to their rapidly emerging real-world applications, such as autonomous driving vehicles, visual surveillance, video retrieval, and entertainment, amongst others. Many efforts have been made over the last few decades to develop a robust and effective framework for action recognition and prediction [34] (Fig. 4.8).

Fig. 4.8 An example of action sequential frames about pick-up

Despite significant progress in human action recognition and prediction, there are still several challenges needed to be further addressed for this task. The first is the diversity of the person, which results that one action category may contain a variety of styles of human movements of various people. Furthermore, videos of the same action can be captured from various perspectives, which also increase the variations of the appearance and the posture. The complexity of the background also can confuse the algorithm in correctly extracting the feature of the human region, which is inevitably encoded the background noise. The movement of the camera is also a common factor that can increase the recognition difficulty because it may cause blurry pictures and loss of motion. In addition, the existing action recognition approaches have demonstrated impressive performance on some small-scale datasets in laboratory settings, the generalization of them in real-world applications still presents a big challenge due to their inability to train on large-scale datasets. Due to the diversity and complexity of the human action, one dataset is also difficult to cover all types of actions. Therefore, the semi-supervised or self-supervised methods should be further investigated to leverage the labelled and unlabelled data from various datasets. Furthermore, a unified action corpus is also necessary to clearly categorize the various types of actions, which is beneficial to develop a more generalized action recognition and prediction method.

4.3.1 Spatial–temporal-Based Action Recognition

The traditional action recognition usually includes two components: representation module and classification module, and a variety of representation method have been proposed, such as the motion energy image, motion history image, space-time interest points, 3D SIFT, etc. The deep learning-based methods combine these two components into a unified end-to-end trainable framework and achieve the state-of-the-art performance. The typical approach is the spatial-temporal-based network,

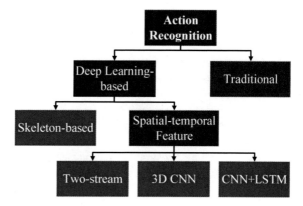

Fig. 4.9 Taxonomy of the action recognition methods

which utilizes the convolutional modules in multi-stream networks to model both appearance and motion information in action videos. The other approach is to utilize the human skeleton information, as the above section discussed, to recognize the corresponding action (Fig. 4.9).

The two-stream structure is a classic spatial–temporal-based method that employs RGB images and optical flow maps. It is firstly proposed by the [35], which utilized a convolutional architecture with two streams that incorporates spatial and temporal networks. The adopted model, that trained on multi-frame dense optical flow, can achieve very good performance despite limited training data. It also shows that multi-task learning can be used to increase the amount of training data whilst improving performance on both when applied to two different action classification datasets. Wang et al. [36] combined a sparse temporal sampling strategy with video-level supervision to allow for efficient and effective learning with the entire action video, a temporal segment network is proposed for action recognition, which is founded on the concept of long-term temporal structure modelling. Carreira et al. [37] presented a new Two-Stream Inflated 3D CNN (I3D) based on 2D convolutional network inflation, where the filters and pooling kernels have been expanded into 3D, allowing for the learning of seamless spatial–temporal feature extractors from video whilst leveraging successful ImageNet architecture designs and even their parameters.

Besides the optical flow, the 3D CNN is introduced by the [38], which demonstrated that the 3D CNN is better suitable for learning spatial–temporal features than 2D CNN, and it is also verified in the [39]. Furthermore, Tran et al. [39] found that splitting the 3D convolutional filters into separate spatial and temporal components results in significant accuracy gains. Their empirical research leads to the development of a new spatiotemporal convolutional block "$R(2 + 1)D$," which produces CNNs with results comparable to or better than the state-of-the-art performance. To alleviate the high computational costs and memory requirements of a deep 3D CNN model from scratch results, Qiu et al. [40] reused the off-the-shelf 2D networks and proposed a Pseudo-3D Residual Net, which exploits all variants of blocks but composes each in a different placement of Residual Net, based on the philosophy that increasing structural diversity whilst going deep can improve the power of neural networks. The optimization of the 3D CNN structure is further investigated in [41, 42], which aims to discover a more efficient approach that leverages the appearance and motion information.

As the previous chapter discussed, the LSTM is a typical model that can tackle sequential inputs because they can directly map variable length inputs to variable length outputs and model complex temporal dynamics whilst being optimized with backpropagation. Therefore, it can be utilized to handle the action recognition combined with the CNN model which is used to extract the spatial features. Donahue et al. [43] proposed a novel recurrent convolutional architecture that is end-to-end trainable and suitable for large-scale visual learning, and they demonstrated the value of these models on benchmark video recognition tasks, image to sentence generation problems, and video narration challenges. When non-linearities are incorporated into network state updates, it is possible to learn long-term dependencies.

4.3.2 Skeleton-Based Action Recognition

The previous section has discussed the advancement of human pose estimation, which has shown the promising results in various benchmarks. Leveraging the skeleton information instead of the raw image is an intuitive idea, where we can take advantage of the skeleton to filter out the complex and dynamic background and focus on the human action itself. Each action can be presented by a sequence of skeleton poses. To classify actions, Weng et al. [44] proposed a Spatio-Temporal-NBNN model, which uses stage-to-class distance. The ST-NBNN, in particular, uses bilinear classifiers to identify key temporal stages as well as spatial joints for action classification. Furthermore, Weng et al. [45] introduce a one-dimensional convolution neural network, called Deformable Pose Traversal Convolution, to represent 3D pose rather than directly representing it using its joint locations. It can extract pose features by identifying key joint combinations, which can then be interpreted for action and gesture comprehension. The ConvLSTM [46] is used to learn the deformation offsets of the convolution kernel and simulates the temporal dynamics of key joint combinations. The emerging graph neural network (GNN) also promotes some researchers to introduce it into action recognition. Yan et al. [47] proposed a new model of dynamic skeletons called Spatial Temporal Graph Convolutional Networks, which constructs a set of spatial temporal graph convolutions on the skeleton sequences. The proposed model can overcome previous limitations by automatically learning both spatial and temporal patterns from data, which not only increases expressive power but also generalization capability. The GNN-based method is also a promising direction for skeleton-based action recognition, since the skeleton is a natural graph structure.

4.3.3 Common Datasets

UCF101 [48] is one of the commonly used datasets for action recognition, which is collected from YouTube with 101 action categories. UCF101 has the most diversity in terms of actions, with 13,320 videos from 101 action categories, and it is the most challenging data set to date, with large variations in camera motion, object appearance and pose, object scale, viewpoint, cluttered background, illumination conditions, and so on. Because the majority of available action recognition data sets are unrealistic and staged by actors, UCF101 aims to encourage further action recognition research by learning and exploring new realistic action categories.

Another popular dataset is the HMDB [49], which is compiled from a variety of sources, the majority of which were movies, with a small portion coming from public databases such as the Prelinger archive, YouTube, and Google videos. The dataset contains 6849 clips organized into 51 action categories, each with at least 101 clips. The action categories are classified into five types: general facial actions, facial actions with object manipulation, general body movements, body movements with object interaction, and body movements for human interaction.

Kinetics-700 [50] is also a commonly used dataset, which has a total of 650,000-clip videos that cover 700 human action classes. Human–object interactions, as well as human–human interactions, are depicted in the videos. There are at least 700 video clips in each action class. Each clip lasts about 10 s and is annotated with an action class.

Besides the above datasets, the other open-source datasets have Moment in Time [51], and 20BN-SOMETHING-SOMETHING [52]. The readers can choose the appropriate dataset according to the specific purpose.

4.4 Vision-Based Body Reconstruction

The purpose of vision-based human body reconstruction is to recover the 3D geometry and appearance of humans from images, videos, or depth maps. The main challenge is to achieve accurate, efficient, and photorealistic human reconstruction and re-rendering using portable and affordable devices. This field has recently been revisited with increased attention due to the development of computational hardware and deep learning technology. The broad application scenarios have also promoted its progress, and the potential applications include VR/AR, file production, free-viewpoint videos, telepresence, sports broadcasting, entertainment, and gaming [53].

The traditional reconstruction usually takes it as a fusion and optimization task, which usually needs a well-designed capture system to ensure the quality of the reconstructed model. However, this kind of approach is time-consuming, and the device is usually expensive, limiting its promotion. Moreover, it is hard to tackle the dynamic human. Some studies attempt to utilize the commercial depth sensor and combine with the human pose and prior to track the dynamic human, which does not fundamentally address the problem of its limited application scenarios.

To reconstruct the 3d human model from a single or sparse-view image, some studies put the attention on leveraging the human prior. The concept behind is that the human can infer human geometry only from a single image. The reason is that humans have prior experience with the human body. The proposal of the SMPL has exploded this field. The SMPL has been introduced in the previous section, which is a parametric 3d human model. Its shape and pose can be changed by a few parameters. Therefore, a lot of SMPL-based methods have been presented, which aim to estimate the driven parameters and obtain a coarse body mesh.

With the development of the deep learning technology, the learning-based method has become a hot research spot. Compared with the fusion-based method and model-based method, it theoretically can achieve a more accurate and photo-realistic model. The learning-based approach aims to learn the implicit representation from the training samples. However, it is limited by the generalization, and usually relies on a large annotation dataset. The emerging neural radiance field (NeRF) [54] has achieved impressive performance in rendering the 3D scene, which also inspires the related researcher to introduce it into the human reconstruction. We think it is the most promising and exciting direction.

4.4.1 Model-Based Reconstruction

The model-based method aims to leverage the learned human prior to reconstruct the 3d human model from a single or sparse-view image. A substantial amount of work has been done using a deep learning-based approach, in which neural networks are trained to infer human models from the annotated datasets, which attempt to obtain the various representations, such as meshes, voxels, and implicit functions, which can be utilized for the network output. The proposal of the SMPL model is a milestone progress and has exploded this field. The SMPL is a statistically parametric 3d human model that can be deformed to fit the shape and pose of various people by controlling a few parameters [16]. The SMPL-based method has become significant and represented the approach of the model-based studies, which typically utilized the SMPL as a geometric prior and exploit its low dimensionality representative vector to drive and generate the coarse body meshes from images. Therefore, it is often accompanied by human pose estimation, where various networks are trained to regress the regress model driven parameters by minimizing the reprojection error between model-based and annotator-based 2D joint positions [55, 56], human segmentation masks and 3D volume projections [57, 58] or body parts [59, 60]. Leveraging its powerful expressive ability, the 3d human model can be inferred from just a single image, which promotes it can be utilized in a wide range of applications. However, its limitation is clear, which is hard to obtain the photorealistic model.

4.4.2 Fusion-Based Reconstruction

The fusion-based method is the traditional approach for constructing the human body model. To achieve an accurate and realistic result, it usually requires a well-designed and sophisticated capture system, such as dense camera arrays, specific markers, high precision Lidar, etc. It entails calibration, fusion, and optimization of multi-view cameras, which must deal with massive amounts of data and necessitate the use of expensive computational resources, resulting in an extremely computationally time-consuming process that is difficult to handle dynamic human activity in real time [61]. The complex capture systems and utilized expensive devices severely limit the promotion of the traditional fusion-based human reconstruction (Fig. 4.10).

To alleviate these problems, some studies put their attention on the commercial depth sensors to achieve real-time reconstruction by fusing the depth maps. The seminal work is made by Newcombe et al. [62], who proposed a dense simultaneous localization and mapping (SLAM)-based reconstruction framework called DynamicFusion, which can reconstruct non-rigidly deforming scenes in real time by fusing RGBD maps captured from commodity sensors, whilst simultaneously estimating a dense volumetric 6D motion field that warps the estimated geometry into a live frame. To tackle the highly dynamic human motion, DoubleFusion [63] is proposed by combing the human skeleton and shape priors, where a double layer representation is proposed which consists of a complete parametric body shape inside and a gradually fused outer surface layer. A pre-defined node graph on the body surface parameterizes non-rigid deformations close to the body, whilst a free-form dynamically changing graph parameterizes the outer surface layer far from the body, allowing for more general reconstruction.

The general pipeline of the fusion-based method can be summarized as shown in Fig. 4.10. The key step is the fusion module, which relies on a robust objective optimization function. To accelerate the converging of the optimization, some constraints usually need to be assumed, resulting in limited application scenarios. Since it is an optimization task, local optimal fusion results are inevitable, which will affect the final reconstruction performance. In addition, the quality of the depth sensor used also has a significant impact on this issue. However, the advancement of the fusion-based method is not ignored, and it plays an important role in the progress of human body reconstruction.

Fig. 4.10 The general pipeline of the fusion-based reconstruction method

4.4.3 Neural Rendering-Based Reconstruction

With the rapid development of deep learning technology, the neural network-based approach for human body reconstruction has been investigated to leverage its powerful representation capability. To utilize the neural network, an appropriate representation of the model should be explored to meet the suitable output form of the network. The voxel-based representation has been firstly investigated, it can be found in the works of [58, 64]. However, the big challenge of the voxel model is the high computational memory consuming, especially when obtaining a high-quality output model. Therefore, the researchers have put their attention on the implicit representations. The typical study is the Pixel-aligned Implicit Function (PIFu) [65], which proposed an implicit representation that aligns pixels in 2D images with the global context of their corresponding 3D object locally. An end-to-end deep learning method is presented for digitizing highly detailed clothed humans, which can infer both 3D surfaces and texture from a single image and, optionally, multiple-input images leveraging PIFu. Unlike the voxel representation, it is memory efficient and can handle arbitrary topology, and the resulting surface is spatially aligned with the input image to achieve the photorealistic result. However, its generalization capability is limited because it relies on the larger and well-established annotated dataset. These critical issues should be further investigated for broader application. Recently, the emerging neural rendering technology has attracted numerous attentions, which can reconstruct the scene directly from multiple images by learning the implicit representation of the scenario without an explicit model. The representative NeRF [54] has presented the remarkable performance in novel view synthesis of the static scenario. Peng et al. [66] introduced the NeRF into the human body reconstruction combined with the SMPL model, which enables the dynamic human reconstruction from sparse views. Peng et al. [67] utilized the linear blending scheme to reconstruct animatable human models from sparse multi-view videos leveraging the NeRF. Due to the impressive performance of the neural rendering-based methods, it should be the most promising research direction and topic in the next period.

4.5 Summary

The chapter has systematically sorted out the popular human body-related activity recognition tasks, including body pose estimation, action recognition, and body reconstruction. The related sub-tasks are also introduced, and the corresponding state-of-the-art methods are discussed. As an important interaction cue, it has broad application scenarios. Therefore, it has attracted considerable attention to improve the accuracy, efficiency, and robustness of the recognition and address the challenges of the diversity and complexity of the human body activity. The advancement of deep learning and computer vision technology has furthered promoted its progress, and various learning-based approaches are proposed and have achieved impressive performance, which should be a promising direction for this field. According to the previous discussion, it can also be found that the different tasks have interrelationships, such as the body pose estimation can be served to support the action recognition and the body reconstruction. In the further, we can further explore their implicit and explicit relation and investigate the unified approach.

References

1. Maurer U, Smailagic A, Siewiorek DP, Deisher M (2008) Activity recognition and monitoring using multiple sensors on different body positions. In: International workshop on wearable and implantable body sensor networks (BSN'06). IEEE, p 4
2. Pang Y, Yuan Y, Li X, Pan J (2011) Efficient hog human detection. Signal Process 91(4):773–781
3. Sun K, Xiao B, Liu D, Wang J (2019) Deep high-resolution representation learning for human pose estimation. In: Proceedings of the IEEE/CVF conference on computer vision and pattern recognition, pp 5693–5703
4. Amin S, Andriluka M, Rohrbach M, Schiele B (2013) Multi-view pictorial structures for 3d human pose estimation. In: BMVC, vol 1
5. Hofmann M, Gavrila DM (2012) Multi-view 3d human pose estimation in complex environment. Int J Comput Vision 96(1):103–124
6. Rafi U, Gall J, Leibe B (2015) A semantic occlusion model for human pose estimation from a single depth image. In: Proceedings of the IEEE conference on computer vision and pattern recognition workshops, pp 67–74
7. Yub Jung H, Lee S, Seok Heo Y, Dong Yun, I (2015) Random tree walk toward instantaneous 3d human pose estimation. In: Proceedings of the IEEE conference on computer vision and pattern recognition, pp 2467–2474
8. Tekin B, Rozantsev A, Lepetit V, Fua P (2016) Direct prediction of 3d body poses from motion compensated sequences. In: Proceedings of the IEEE conference on computer vision and pattern recognition, pp 991–1000
9. Zhou X, Zhu M, Leonardos S, Derpanis KG, Daniilidis K (2016) Sparseness meets deepness: 3d human pose estimation from monocular video. In: Proceedings of the IEEE conference on computer vision and pattern recognition, p. 4966–4975
10. Ramakrishna V, Kanade T, Sheikh Y (2012) Reconstructing 3d human pose from 2d image landmarks. In: European conference on computer vision. Springer, pp 573–586
11. Wang C, Wang Y, Lin Z, Yuille AL, Gao W (2014) Robust estimation of 3d human poses from a single image. In: Proceedings of the IEEE conference on computer vision and pattern recognition, pp 2361–2368
12. Akhter I, Black MJ (2015) Pose-conditioned joint angle limits for 3d human pose reconstruction. In: Proceedings of the IEEE conference on computer vision and pattern recognition, pp 1446–1455
13. Simo-Serra E, Ramisa A, Alenyà G, Torras C, Moreno-Noguer F (2012) Single image 3d human pose estimation from noisy observations. In: 2012 IEEE conference on computer vision and pattern recognition. IEEE, pp 2673–2680
14. Wei XK, Chai J (2009) Modeling 3d human poses from uncalibrated monocular images. In: 2009 IEEE 12th International conference on computer vision. IEEE, pp 1873–1880
15. Chen C-H, Ramanan D (2017) 3d human pose estimation = 2d pose estimation+ matching. In: Proceedings of the IEEE conference on computer vision and pattern recognition, pp 7035–7043
16. Loper M, Mahmood N, Romero J, Pons-Moll G, Black MJ (2015) Smpl: A skinned multi-person linear model. ACM Trans Graph (TOG) 34(6):1–16

17. Bogo F, Kanazawa A, Lassner C, Gehler P, Romero J, Black MJ (2016) Keep it SMPL: automatic estimation of 3d human pose and shape from a single image. In: European conference on computer vision. Springer, pp 561–578
18. Pishchulin L, Insafutdinov E, Tang S, Andres B, Andriluka M, Gehler PV, Schiele B (2016) Deepcut: joint subset partition and labeling for multi person pose estimation. In: Proceedings of the IEEE conference on computer vision and pattern recognition, pp 4929–4937
19. Insafutdinov E, Pishchulin L, Andres B, Andriluka M, Schiele B (2016) Deepercut: a deeper, stronger, and faster multi-person pose estimation model. In: European conference on computer vision, Springer, pp 34–50
20. Johnson S, Everingham M (2010) Clustered pose and nonlinear appearance models for human pose estimation. In: BMVC, vol 2, p 5
21. Cao Z, Simon T, Wei S-E, Sheikh Y (2017) Realtime multi-person 2d pose estimation using part affinity fields. In: Proceedings of the IEEE conference on computer vision and pattern recognition, pp 7291–7299
22. Sapp B, Taskar B (2013) MODEC: Multimodal decomposable models for human pose estimation. In: Proceedings of the IEEE conference on computer vision and pattern recognition, pp 3674–3681
23. Andriluka M, Pishchulin L, Gehler P, Schiele B (2014) 2d human pose estimation: new benchmark and state of the art analysis. In: Proceedings of the IEEE conference on computer vision and pattern recognition, pp 3686–3693
24. Lin T-Y, Maire M, Belongie S, Hays J, Perona P, Ramanan D, Dollár P, Zitnick CL (2014) Microsoft coco: Common objects in context. In: European conference on computer vision. Springer, pp 740–755
25. Andriluka M, Iqbal U, Insafutdinov E, Pishchulin L, Milan A, Gall J, Schiele B (2018) Pose-Track: a benchmark for human pose estimation and tracking. In: Proceedings of the IEEE conference on computer vision and pattern recognition, pp 5167–5176
26. Ionescu C, Papava D, Olaru V, Sminchisescu C (2014) Human3.6m: large scale datasets and predictive methods for 3d human sensing in natural environments. IEEE Trans Pattern Anal Mach Intell 36(7):1325–1339
27. Sigal L, Balan AO, Black MJ (2010) Humaneva: synchronized video and motion capture dataset and baseline algorithm for evaluation of articulated human motion. Int J Comput Vision 87(1):4–27
28. Joo H, Simon T, Cikara M, Sheikh Y (2019) Towards social artificial intelligence: nonverbal social signal prediction in a triadic interaction. In: CVPR
29. Fabbri M Lanzi F, Calderara S, Palazzi A, Vezzani R, Cucchiara R (2018) Learning to detect and track visible and occluded body joints in a virtual world. In: European conference on computer vision (ECCV)
30. Mehta D, Rhodin H, Casas D, Fua P, Sotnychenko O, Xu W, Theobalt C (20) Monocular 3d human pose estimation in the wild using improved cnn supervision. In: 2017 Fifth international conference on 3D vision (3DV). IEEE.https://doi.org/10.1109/3dv.2017.00064, http://gvv.mpi-inf.mpg.de/3dhpdataset
31. Varol G, Romero J, Martin X, Mahmood N, Black MJ, Laptev I, Schmid C (2017) Learning from synthetic humans. In: CVPR
32. Lassner C, Romero J, Kiefel M, Bogo F, Black MJ, Gehler PV (2017) Unite the people: closing the loop between 3d and 2d human representations. In: Proceedings of the IEEE conference on computer vision and pattern recognition, pp 6050–6059
33. Riza Alp Guler IK Neverova N (2018) DensePose: Dense human pose estimation in the wild
34. Kong Y, Fu, Y (2018) Human action recognition and prediction: a survey. arXiv:1806.11230
35. Simonyan K, Zisserman A (2014) Two-stream convolutional networks for action recognition in videos. In: Advances in neural information processing systems, vol 27
36. Wang L, Xiong Y, Wang Z, Qiao Y, Lin D, Tang X, Gool LV (2016) Temporal segment networks: Towards good practices for deep action recognition. In: European conference on computer vision. Springer, pp 20–36

37. Carreira J, Zisserman A (2017) Quo vadis, action recognition? a new model and the kinetics dataset. In: Proceedings of the IEEE conference on computer vision and pattern recognition, pp 6299–6308
38. Tran D, Bourdev L, Fergus R, Torresani L, Paluri M (2015) Learning spatiotemporal features with 3d convolutional networks. In: Proceedings of the IEEE international conference on computer vision, pp 4489–4497
39. Tran, D, Wang, H, Torresani, L, Ray, J, LeCun, Y, Paluri, M (2018) A closer look at spatiotemporal convolutions for action recognition. In: Proceedings of the IEEE conference on computer vision and pattern recognition (CVPR)
40. Qiu Z, Yao T, Mei T (2017) Learning spatio-temporal representation with pseudo-3d residual networks. In: Proceedings of the IEEE international conference on computer vision (ICCV)
41. Zolfaghari M, Singh K, Brox T (2018) Eco: efficient convolutional network for online video understanding. In: Proceedings of the European conference on computer vision (ECCV), pp 695–712
42. Crasto N, Weinzaepfel P, Alahari K, Schmid C (2019) MARS: Motion-augmented RGB stream for action recognition. In: Proceedings of the IEEE/CVF conference on computer vision and pattern recognition, pp 7882–7891
43. Donahue J, Anne Hendricks L, Guadarrama S, Rohrbach M, Venugopalan S, Saenko K, Darrell T (2015) Long-term recurrent convolutional networks for visual recognition and description. In: Proceedings of the IEEE conference on computer vision and pattern recognition, pp 2625–2634
44. Weng J, Weng C, Yuan J (2017) Spatio-temporal Naive-Bayes nearest-neighbor (ST-NBNN) for skeleton-based action recognition. In: Proceedings of the IEEE conference on computer vision and pattern recognition (CVPR)
45. Weng J, Liu M, Jiang X, Yuan J (2018) Deformable pose traversal convolution for 3d action and gesture recognition. In: Proceedings of the European conference on computer vision (ECCV)
46. Shi X, Chen Z, Wang H, Yeung D-Y, Wong W-K, Woo W-C (2015) Convolutional LSTM network: a machine learning approach for precipitation nowcasting. In: Advances in neural information processing systems, vol 28
47. Yan S, Xiong Y, Lin D (2018) Spatial temporal graph convolutional networks for skeleton-based action recognition. In: Thirty-second AAAI conference on artificial intelligence
48. Soomro K, Zamir AR, Shah M (2012) Ucf101: a dataset of 101 human actions classes from videos in the wild. arXiv:1212.0402
49. Kuehne H, Jhuang H, Garrote E, Poggio T, Serre T (2011) HMDB: a large video database for human motion recognition. In: 2011 International conference on computer vision. IEEE, pp 2556–2563
50. Smaira L, Carreira J, Noland E, Clancy E, Wu A, Zisserman A (2020) A short note on the kinetics-700-2020 human action dataset. arXiv:2010.10864
51. Monfort M, Andonian A, Zhou B, Ramakrishnan K, Bargal SA, Yan T, Brown L, Fan Q, Gutfruend D, Vondrick C et al (2019) Moments in time dataset: one million videos for event understanding. IEEE Trans Pattern Anal Mach Intell 1–8
52. Goyal R, Ebrahimi Kahou S, Michalski V, Materzynska J, Westphal S, Kim H, Haenel V, Fruend I, Yianilos P, Mueller-Freitag M, et al (2017) The "something something" video database for learning and evaluating visual common sense. In: Proceedings of the IEEE international conference on computer vision, pp 5842–5850
53. Chen L, Peng S, Zhou X (2021) Towards efficient and photorealistic 3d human reconstruction: a brief survey. Vis Inform 5(4):11–19
54. Mildenhall B, Srinivasan PP, Tancik M, Barron JT, Ramamoorthi R, Ng R (2020) NeRf: representing scenes as neural radiance fields for view synthesis. In: European conference on computer vision. Springer, pp 405–421
55. Kanazawa A, Black MJ, Jacobs DW, Malik J (2018) End-to-end recovery of human shape and pose. In: Proceedings of the IEEE conference on computer vision and pattern recognition (CVPR)
56. Tung H-Y, Tung H-W, Yumer E, Fragkiadaki K (2017) Self-supervised learning of motion capture. In: Guyon I, Luxburg UV, Bengio S, Wallach H, Fergus R, Vishwanathan S, Garnett R (eds) Advances in neural information processing systems, vol 30. Curran Associates, Inc

57. Tung H-YF, Harley AW, Seto W, Fragkiadaki K (2017) Adversarial inverse graphics networks: learning 2d-to-3d lifting and image-to-image translation from unpaired supervision. In: 2017 IEEE international conference on computer vision (ICCV), pp 4364–4372

58. Varol G, Ceylan D, Russell B, Yang J, Yumer E, Laptev I, Schmid C (2018) BodyNet: volumetric inference of 3d human body shapes. In: Proceedings of the European conference on computer vision (ECCV)

59. Omran M Lassner C, Pons-Moll G, Gehler P, Schiele B (2018) Neural body fitting: unifying deep learning and model based human pose and shape estimation. In: 2018 international conference on 3D vision (3DV), pp 484–494

60. Guler RA, Kokkinos I (2019) HoloPose: Holistic 3d human reconstruction in-the-wild. In: Proceedings of the IEEE/CVF conference on computer vision and pattern recognition (CVPR)

61. Guo K, Lincoln P, Davidson P, Busch J, Yu X, Whalen M, Harvey G, Orts-Escolano S, Pandey R, Dourgarian J et al (2019) The relightables: volumetric performance capture of humans with realistic relighting. ACM Trans Graph (ToG) 38(6):1–19

62. Newcombe RA, Fox D, Seitz SM (2015) DynamicFusion: reconstruction and tracking of non-rigid scenes in real-time. In: Proceedings of the IEEE conference on computer vision and pattern recognition (CVPR)

63. Yu T, Zheng Z, Guo K, Zhao J, Dai Q, Li H, Pons-Moll G, Liu Y (2018) Doublefusion: real-time capture of human performances with inner body shapes from a single depth sensor. In: Proceedings of the IEEE conference on computer vision and pattern recognition (CVPR)

64. Zheng Z, Yu T, Wei Y, Dai Q, Liu Y (2019) DeepHuman: 3d human reconstruction from a single image. In: Proceedings of the IEEE/CVF international conference on computer vision (ICCV)

65. Saito S, Huang Z, Natsume R, Morishima S, Kanazawa A, Li H (2019) PIFu: pixel-aligned implicit function for high-resolution clothed human digitization. In: Proceedings of the IEEE/CVF international conference on computer vision (ICCV)

66. Peng S, Zhang Y, Xu Y, Wang Q, Shuai Q, Bao H, Zhou X (2021) Neural body: implicit neural representations with structured latent codes for novel view synthesis of dynamic humans. In: Proceedings of the IEEE/CVF conference on computer vision and pattern recognition (CVPR), pp 9054–9063

67. Peng S, Dong J, Wang Q, Zhang S, Shuai Q, Bao H, Zhou X (2021) Animatable neural radiance fields for human body modeling. arXiv eprints, 2105

Chapter 5
Vision-Based Human Attention Modelling

Abstract This chapter is primarily concerned with human attention modelling, specifically the human driver. Previous related studies have typically focused on a single side without providing a comprehensive understanding. As a result, this chapter introduces a context-aware human driver attention estimation framework that combines scene visual saliency information and appearance-based driver state to provide a more accurate estimation. It has been validated in a VR-based experimental platform. Currently, the implicit and explicit of the human cognitive state and the contextual scenario still ill-defined, and we hope the related research can investigate it further.

5.1 Introduction

The previous chapters have discussed the external human activity recognition. Human attention, on the other hand, can be thought of as an internal activity associated with the human cognitive state. However, it can be reflected in human external states such as head posture, gaze direction, body posture, and so on. A common approach is also to use the external state to infer attention. Human attention modelling is an important task to construct the harmonious human–machine system, especially for the intelligent vehicle which will play an important role in our daily lives. This chapter will utilize the human driver as the main research object to discuss the attention modelling. The SAE [1] divides autonomous driving into six categories. Whilst the future of autonomous driving looks promising, mainstream vehicles are still a few years away from reaching Level 5 (full automation). Semi-autonomous driving will be around for quite some time. The perception and understanding of the driver will be a critical task to improve the driving safety, comfort, and intelligence, where the human driver attention modelling will be an important function for constructing the advanced driver assistance system.

The purpose of human attention modelling is to obtain the interest area in a scene, as shown in Fig. 5.1, which indicates the human driver interest area in driving. Human attention is basically comprised of two components: the human and the

Fig. 5.1 Human driver
attention map

contextual scenario. As a result, various studies have investigated it from different perspectives. Some studies focus on the human side, which includes fatigue detection [2], head pose estimation [3], gaze direction estimation [4], and behaviour detection [5]. The driving attention can be judged by recognizing a specific state or posture of the human driver, including whether the driver is distracted, whether the driver's attention is focused on the road, and whether the driver is doing something unrelated to the driving task [6]. Some studies pay attention on the scenario and investigate the effects of various scenarios on the driver's attention [7]. A saliency map is typically estimated to estimate the potential area that may catch the driver's attention [8]. Due to the scene changes dynamically, the human driver usually pays attention to a few salient areas. As a result, the human driver's attention is drawn to the saliency map. The saliency map, on the other hand, is subject to subjectivity and individuality. Different human drivers may pay attention to different areas of the same image due to their different tasks and habits. With the advancement of deep learning, many researchers began to view attention evaluation as a data-driven problem.

The deep learning-based model can estimate the potential area of an image by setting scenes and tasks and collecting a large amount of data. The DY(eye)VE project [9] is a representative study in which an open video dataset with human driver eye tracking is built and a deep learning model is able to replicate the human driver's attentional behaviour during driving tasks. Several researchers are also attempting to map the relationship between the human driver's posture (gaze and head posture) and the external environment. The primary research task is gaze zone estimation [10–12], which divides various areas from the human driver's perspective, such as front-view glass, centre console, instrument panel, left and right rear-view mirrors, and so on. Some researchers furtherly divide the front-view glass into additional areas, which usually necessitate calibration.

5.2 Visual Saliency Map Estimation

In general, there are two types of saliency estimation methods: task-free methods and task-driven methods [14]. The goal of task-free approaches is to determine the

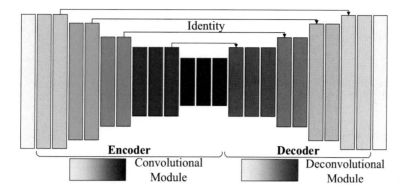

Fig. 5.2 The typical encoder–decoder structure for saliency map estimation

saliency area of a general scene. Traditional methods use a bottom-up approach to extract various levels of visual features such as colour, intensity, and orientation [15–18]. The success of deep learning models, particularly CNNs, has demonstrated their significant potential in a wide range of image-based applications. Many deep learning-enabled saliency models have been proposed in recent years, and they have been shown to outperform traditional approaches. The encoder–decoder model architecture is the most commonly used model architecture [19, 20], which adheres to the idea of traditional methods. The model can learn to extract saliency features by deepening the network and expanding the receptive field. To avoid network degradation, a skip connection is utilized between the encoder and decoder layers to form a symmetric structure [21, 22], as shown in Fig. 5.2.

Approaches based on task-driven saliency estimation seek scene information related to an ongoing task. This chapter focuses on driving scenarios. The first challenge is to create a dataset for estimating driving saliency. Palazzi et al. [9] developed the largest dataset, DR(eye)VE, to predict driver attention; this dataset also includes a multi-branch network to handle multiple inputs. This dataset has two major flaws: driving-personalized protocol and driving-irrelevant data. To address these shortcomings, Xia et al. [23] proposed the Berkeley deep drive attention (BDD-A) dataset, which collects the gaze of multiple observers in a lab. The critical driving video in [23] was chosen from the BDD-A dataset based on braking events. A pre-trained AlexNet and a convolutional long short-term memory network were used to create the proposed model. A traffic-driving dataset containing the gaze data of multiple drivers was created in [24], and a convolutional–deconvolutional neural network (CDNN) was also proposed to predict driving saliency using bottom-up and top-down approaches. The same encoder–decoder structure was used in [25, 26]. A conditional generative adversarial network (GAN) was proposed in [27] to generate the saliency map, and a visual attention driving database based on existing driving datasets was introduced. In [28], a driving accident dataset was used to build driver attention, and semantic information was used to predict driver attention using a proposed two-stream network. In [29] used inverse reinforcement learning to predict the driver attention areas with the highest rewards.

5.3 Context-Aware Human Attention Estimation

5.3.1 Methodology

The existing studies usually focused on a single aspect, such as the human driver or the scenario saliency, without taking a comprehensive approach. This is completely unreasonable. To address these issues, this chapter introduces a context-aware human driver attention estimation framework that takes into account not only the saliency map of the contextual scenario but also the driver's gaze, as shown in Fig. 5.3. This is also one of the most significant differences between the introduced context-aware attention estimation method and others in the field. The gaze is a cue that can directly expresses the human driver's attention and can be extracted from the driver's face using non-invasive computer vision technology without the use of a specific eye-tracking device. To integrate the gaze direction and the saliency map, a gaze probability map is introduced to transform the gaze direction into a feature map that can indicate the different responses of the various area. Due to the introduced method assumes that the gaze and scene image are not calibrated, a CNN-based network is utilized as a data-driven solution to address the challenge.

The studies that focus on the driver side usually need calibrations to establish a mapping model with the environment. These methods, however, are easily influenced by different types and locations of human drivers. Yang et al. [30], for example, utilized several markers to calibrate the transformation relationship between the driver and the camera, but as the driver's position changes, so does the transformation relationship. Palazzi et al. [9] captured gaze data using commercial eye tracking

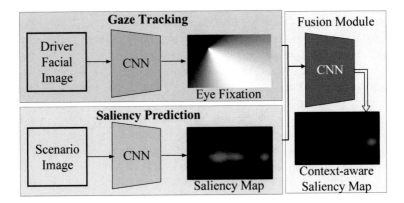

Fig. 5.3 The framework of the context-aware human driver attention estimation

glasses and performed image registration between the glasses' egocentric camera and the roof-mounted front-view camera, and they only use the eye tracking glasses during the data collection stage. In comparison, the book prefers the non-invasive computer vision method.

Eye gaze is an important non-verbal cue for estimating human attention. There are numerous works in computer vision for gaze estimation as previous chapter discussed. It has used in a variety of applications like affective computing and human–robot interaction. The most recent appearance-based methods, which employ convolutional neural networks, have more robust performance that is not limited to lighting and appearance variation. On open datasets such as the MPIIGaze dataset, the accuracy of the state-of-the-art methods for gaze estimation can achieve 4°–5°, which promotes us to utilize the data-driven approach. In addition, calibration between the two is difficult without the use of eye-tracking glasses is a challenging task. As a result, this section proposes the gaze probability map, which is used to establish a calibration-free relationship between the gaze vector and the front-view image. The pixel value $I_g(x, y)$ of the probability map location (x, y) is as follows:

$$I_g(x, y) = v \cdot (x - \alpha, y - \beta)/(x - \alpha, y - \beta) \tag{5.1}$$

$$(\alpha, \beta) = (\alpha_0, \beta_0) + \neg v * 0.1 * n \tag{5.2}$$

where v denotes the normalized gaze direction, $\neg v$ is the inverse vector of the normalized gaze direction, (α, β) indicates the adjusted starting location of the gaze, and (α_0, β_0) represents the approximate position of the eye relative to the front-view image, and the value range is 0–1. The n is (w, h), which is equal to the image's size. This can cause the (α, β) to be offset in the opposite direction of the. The goal of the above equation is to broaden the effective range of the probability map and avoid the negative effects caused by the (α_0, β_0).

Given that the gaze probability map and scene saliency map belong to two distinct views in the absence of calibration, it is difficult to simply merge them with a specific weight or paradigm. The deep neural network, on the other hand, provides an efficient method for making the weights learnable. Deep neural networks have powerful learning capabilities as a data-driven method. It is believed that the key capability of the convolution network is the ability to learn features at different levels, and that these different levels of features contribute differently to the output vector. Therefore, we can leverage an introduced multi-scale CNN model to learn the implicit relationship between the human gaze cue and the scenario saliency.

5.3.2   Model Analysis

The primary goal of this chapter is to introduce a model of the dual-view gaze direction and scene image that will aid in the design of a non-invasive driver attention monitoring system based on computer vision. The most important aspect of the proposed method is determining how to obtain the ground truth. Because of the advancement of virtual reality technology, we no longer need to calibrate the driver's view and the front-view image. We designed a VR-based driving simulator which can obtain the synchronized gaze direction and front-view image, as well as the associated ground truth. In comparison to other solutions, the virtual reality platform can obtain more accurate data because it integrates the driver and the virtual environment into the same world coordinate system. Based on the designed experimental platform, the human driver state is complimented for the DR(eye)VE dataset, which includes 74 video clips collected in various driving scenarios, landscapes, weather conditions, and times.

Several widely used saliency metrics have been analysed in [33]. Based on the MIT Saliency Benchmark, they found that the Pearson's correlation coefficient (CC) metric and normalized scanpath saliency (NSS) provide the fairest comparison under assumptions that all systematic dataset biases are accounted for in the model and the saliency models are not probabilistic. However, if saliency models are considered as probabilistic models, then Kullback–Leibler (KL) divergence and information gain (IG) are recommended.

One of the hypotheses of this chapter is that gaze direction is an important cue for estimating driver attention. To begin, the SalGAN model [31] and the SAM model [32] are utilized to generate the saliency map and serve as the baselines. The SalGAN is a deep convolutional neural network trained with adversarial examples for visual saliency prediction, whereas the core of SAM is a convolutional LSTM that focuses on the most salient regions of the input image to iteratively refine the predicted saliency map. On public saliency prediction datasets, they all achieve state-of-the-art performance across multiple metrics. The gaze probability maps are then used to dot these two saliency maps. The neural network was not used in the first set of experiments to intuitively evaluate the benefit of the gaze direction, as shown in Fig. 5.4. To evaluate these methods comprehensively, different saliency metrics are used. The combination of the gaze probability map can significantly improve positioning accuracy and distribution similarity. Furthermore, the SalGAN model outperforms the SAM model. The SalGAN model will be used to extract the feature map in the following experiments.

To study the performance of the utilized multi-scale CNN model for driver attention estimation, the comparison is shown in Table 5.1. It should be noted that the KL-div and IG are strongly correlated, and both focus on the distribution shape of the final heatmap, not the accuracy of the object position. In contrast, the CC and NSS emphasize the linear correlation between the prediction heatmap and the ground truth. By comparing the baselines, it is clear that the utilized multi-scale model can significantly improve the estimation performance. It's worth noting that the CC and NSS have all improved significantly, but the KL-div and IG haven't changed much. This also confirmed that KL-div and IG are primarily concerned with the shape of the distribution rather than its accuracy.

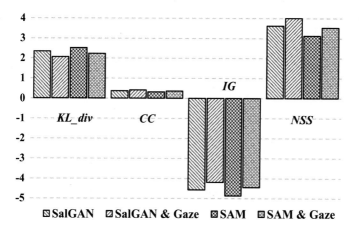

Fig. 5.4 Comparison of the context-aware driver attention estimation and the driving saliency estimation

Table 5.1 The comparison on the DR(eye)VE dataset

Method	KL-div↓	CC↑	IG↑	NSS↑
SalGAN [31]	2.33	0.37	−4.57	3.62
SAM [32]	2.51	0.32	−4.87	3.12
DR(eye)VE [9]	1.41	0.63	−2.63	7.82
SalGAN + Gaze	2.05	0.41	−4.18	4.00
SAM + Gaze	2.22	0.37	−4.46	3.52
Ours	1.73	0.72	−3.19	9.49

↑ represents that the higher value, the better performance. Conversely, ↓ means that the lower value is better

5.4 Summary

Human attention estimation is an important enabling technique to construct the harmonious human–machine system. In this chapter, the human driver is utilized as the research object to evaluate the driver's attention in a driving scenario. Human attention is basically an interaction and cognitive process, which entails the contextual scenario and the human. The previous related studies usually focus on a single side without a comprehensive understanding. Therefore, this chapter introduces a more reasonable and feasible context-aware human driver attention estimation method based on a dual-view calibration-free scene image and eye gaze cue. Visual mechanisms are used to extract low-level saliency features and high-level semantic features from scene images. A gaze probability map is created by transforming the gaze direction. To model them, a data-driven multi-scale CNN model is adopted. Based on a virtual reality experimental platform, the model's performance is evaluated. The experiments show that the introduced method outperforms the baselines on multiple widely used metrics. In the future, we can need to further investigate the implicit cognitive mechanism between the contextual scenario and human attention, which is a critical task to understand the human intention and provide the appropriate assistance and feedback.

References

1. Shadrin SS, Ivanova AA (2019) Analytical review of standard sae j3016 taxonomy and definitions for terms related to driving automation systems for on-road motor vehicles with latest updates. Avtomobil Doroga Infrastruktura 3(21):10
2. Sikander G, Anwar S (2019) Driver fatigue detection systems: a review. IEEE Trans Intell Transp Syst 20(6):2339–2352
3. Hu Z, Zhang Y, Xing Y, Zhao Y, Cao D, Lv C (2022) Toward human-centered automated driving: a novel spatiotemporal vision transformer-enabled head tracker. IEEE Vehi Technol Mag 2–9. https://doi.org/10.1109/MVT.2021.3140047
4. Hu Z, Lv C, Hang P, Huang C, Xing Y (2022) Data-driven estimation of driver attention using calibration-free eye gaze and scene features. IEEE Trans Ind Electron 69(2):1800–1808. https://doi.org/10.1109/TIE.2021.3057033
5. Kashevnik A, Lashkov I, Gurtov A (2020) Methodology and mobile application for driver behavior analysis and accident prevention. IEEE Trans Intell Transp Syst 21(6):2427–2436. https://doi.org/10.1109/TITS.2019.2918328
6. Chiou C-Y, Wang W-C, Lu S-C, Huang C-R, Chung P-C, Lai Y-Y (2020) Driver monitoring using sparse representation with part-based temporal face descriptors. IEEE Trans Intell Transp Syst 21(1):346–361. https://doi.org/10.1109/TITS.2019.2892155
7. Takahashi H, Ukishima D, Kawamoto K, Hirota K (2007) A study on predicting hazard factors for safe driving. IEEE Trans Ind Electron 54(2):781–789
8. Deng T, Yang K, Li Y, Yan H (2016) Where does the driver look? top-down-based saliency detection in a traffic driving environment. IEEE Trans Intell Transp Syst 17(7):2051–2062
9. Palazzi A, Abati D, Calderara S, Solera F, Cucchiara R (2019) Predicting the driver's focus of attention: The dr(eye)ve project. IEEE Trans Pattern Anal Mach Intell 41(7):1720–1733
10. Vora S, Rangesh A, Trivedi MM (2018) Driver gaze zone estimation using convolutional neural networks: A general framework and ablative analysis. IEEE Trans Intell Veh 3(3):254–265
11. Tawari A, Chen KH, Trivedi MM (2014) Where is the driver looking: Analysis of head, eye and iris for robust gaze zone estimation. In: 17th International IEEE conference on intelligent transportation systems (ITSC), pp 988–994
12. Lundgren M, Hammarstrand L, McKelvey T (2016) Driver-gaze zone estimation using bayesian filtering and gaussian processes. IEEE Trans Intell Transp Syst 17(10):2739–2750
13. Martin S, Vora S, Yuen K, Trivedi MM (2018) Dynamics of driver's gaze: explorations in behavior modeling and maneuver prediction. IEEE Transactions on Intelligent Vehicles 3(2):141–150
14. Borji A (2021) Saliency prediction in the deep learning era: successes and limitations. IEEE Trans Pattern Anal Mach Intell 43(2):679–700. https://doi.org/10.1109/TPAMI.2019.2935715
15. Borji A, Itti L (2012) State-of-the-art in visual attention modeling. IEEE Trans Pattern Anal Mach Intell 35(1):185–207
16. Zhang L, Tong MH, Marks TK, Shan H, Cottrell GW (2008) Sun: a Bayesian framework for saliency using natural statistics. J Vis 8(7):32–32
17. Bruce N, Tsotsos J (2005) Saliency based on information maximization. In: Advances in neural information processing systems, pp 155–162

18. Liu T, Yuan Z, Sun J, Wang J, Zheng N, Tang X, Shum H-Y (2010) Learning to detect a salient object. IEEE Trans Pattern Anal Mach Intell 33(2):353–367

19. Kruthiventi, S.S, Gudisa, V, Dholakiya, J.H, Babu, R.V.: Saliency unified: A deep architecture for simultaneous eye fixation prediction and salient object segmentation. In: Proceedings of the IEEE Conference on Computer Vision and Pattern Recognition, pp. 5781–5790 (2016)

20. Jetley S, Murray N, Vig E (2016) End-to-end saliency mapping via probability distribution prediction. In: Proceedings of the IEEE conference on computer vision and pattern recognition, pp 5753–5761

21. Kümmerer M, Wallis TS, Bethge M (2016) Deepgaze ii: reading fixations from deep features trained on object recognition. arXiv:1610.01563

22. Cornia M, Baraldi L, Serra G, Cucchiara R (2016) A deep multi-level network for saliency prediction. In: 2016 23rd International conference on pattern recognition (ICPR). IEEE, pp 3488–3493

23. Xia Y, Zhang D, Kim J, Nakayama K, Zipser K, Whitney D (2018) Predicting driver attention in critical situations. In: Asian conference on computer vision. Springer, pp 658–674

24. Deng T, Yan H, Qin L, Ngo T, Manjunath B (2019) How do drivers allocate their potential attention? driving fixation prediction via convolutional neural networks. IEEE Trans Intell Transp Syst 21(5):2146–2154

25. Tawari A, Kang B (2017) A computational framework for driver's visual attention using a fully convolutional architecture. In: 2017 IEEE intelligent vehicles symposium (IV). IEEE, pp 887–894

26. Palazzi A, Solera F, Calderara S, Alletto S, Cucchiara R (2017) Learning where to attend like a human driver. In: 2017 IEEE intelligent vehicles symposium (IV). IEEE, pp 920–925

27. Lateef F, Kas M, Ruichek Y (2021) Saliency heat-map as visual attention for autonomous driving using generative adversarial network (GAN). IEEE Trans Intell Transp Syst

28. Fang J, Yan D, Qiao J, Xue J, Yu H (2021) Dada: driver attention prediction in driving accident scenarios. IEEE Trans Intell Transp Syst

29. Baee S, Pakdamanian E, Kim I, Feng L, Ordonez V, Barnes L (2021) MEDIRL: predicting the visual attention of drivers via maximum entropy deep inverse reinforcement learning. In: Proceedings of the IEEE/CVF international conference on computer vision, pp 13178–13188

30. Yang L, Dong K, Dmitruk AJ, Brighton J, Zhao Y (2020) A dual-cameras-based driver gaze mapping system with an application on non-driving activities monitoring. IEEE Trans Intell Transp Syst 21(10):4318–4327

31. Pan J, Ferrer CC, McGuinness K, O'Connor NE, Torres J, Sayrol E, Giro-i-Nieto X (2017) SalGAN: visual saliency prediction with generative adversarial networks. arXiv:1701.01081

32. Cornia M, Baraldi L, Serra G, Cucchiara R (2018) Predicting human eye fixations via an LSTM-based saliency attentive model. IEEE Trans Image Process 27(10):5142–5154

33. Bylinskii Z, Judd T, Oliva A, Torralba A, Durand F (2018) What do different evaluation metrics tell us about saliency models? IEEE Trans Pattern Anal Mach Intell 41(3):740–757

Chapter 6
Conclusions and Recommendations

Abstract Despite the promising achievements introduced in the previous chapters, there are still unsettled issues that hinder the development of human activity recognition. In this chapter, we conclude the current progress and give a discussion on these issues as well as research opportunities in the future.

6.1 Conclusions

With the development of intelligent technology, the increasing numbers of intelligent agents have into our daily lives to collaborate with us. The harmonious human–machine system requires that intelligent agents can correctly understand our various states and attentions, which is essential for providing adaptive and personalized feedback and assistance. The vision-based sensor is a widely deployed component that benefits from its affordable and portable, which can be found in many intelligent devices, including smartphones, autonomous vehicles, intelligent robots, security surveillance systems, etc. Its reliable and stable sensing also promotes progress further. Compared to other modalities, the visual signal has included more information and can provide a lot of cues, which benefits the corresponding perception methods based on it. Therefore, vision-based activity recognition is a mainstream approach, which has attracted numerous attention, and considerable studies have been investigated.

The HAR is a system study, which entails various specific topics. The researchers usually focus on a specific one state or behaviour according to the target applications. The previous chapters have systemically sort out the V-HAR related tasks, including hand activity, facial activity, body activity, and attention modelling. The corresponding sub-topics are also clear elaborated. The V-HAR basically focuses on the external activities that can be inferred from the outside appearance. The concept behind it is to simulate human cognitive processes in human-to-human communication, where humans usually can recognize others' states and infer their attention according to their appearance-based behaviours. Furthermore, the related tasks can be classified into three categories: recognition, estimation, and tracking.

Z. Hu and C. Lv, *Vision-Based Human Activity Recognition*,
SpringerBriefs in Intelligent Systems,
https://doi.org/10.1007/978-981-19-2290-9_6

With the advancement of the deep learning technology, the existing studies of the V-HAR basically utilize the deep learning-based approach in a data-driven way. In particular, the convolutional network has achieved remarkable success and plays a dominant role in vision-based recognition tasks. A variety of CNN-based models have been proposed to tackle the various HAR tasks with impressive performance. The V-HAR could be evolved in line with the development of intelligent technology and advanced sensing. It is definitely a promising and interesting research field. The previous chapters have introduced a series of typical and state-of-the-art models, which will benefit the readers to quickly grasp the current development of the corresponding fields and have a comprehensive understanding.

6.2 Recommendations

Although many impressive achievements have been made for the V-HAR, there are still some unsettled issues and interesting directions that need to be furtherly explored.

1. Unified Multi-Modal Human Activity Modelling

Currently, various types of human activities are being studied from various perspectives for various applications. These works are basically built on some assumptions for the specific task. However, the human activity is usually multi-modal that can have various physical or psychological reactions and activities depending on the diverse contextual scenarios. It should be necessary and feasible to build a unified multi-modal human activity modelling system leveraging the deep learning techniques, which can promote the understanding of the human state and intention.

2. Context-Aware Human Activity Modelling

The human activity and behaviour are typically related to the contextual scenarios. Most of the existing studies investigate human activities in a decoupled way. To construct the intelligent human–machine system, we need to know what types of activity are most likely to occur in a given scenario, as well as how much effort of various scenarios will place on humans. It requires us to build the context-aware human activity model to support the harmonious human–machine system to make appropriate feedback and assistance.

3. Advanced Unsupervised Learning for Human Activity Modelling

The deep learning techniques have shown their powerful learning capability. It is currently the most used approach. However, deep learning-based methods rely on large datasets, and this is a challenge for this field. Especially, a large multi-modal corpus dataset of human activity is lacking. Besides the effort of collecting data, unsupervised learning models are needed to be developed to deal with it. Furthermore, human activity is complex, diverse, and personalized. It is difficult to build a dataset that can cover all situations. Therefore, advanced unsupervised approaches should be further explored to alleviate the dilemma of lack of data.

4. Integration and Fusion of Model-Based and Data-Driven Approaches

The previous chapters have introduced that there are usually two types of approaches for the V-HAR, model-based, and data-driven, due to the human prior knowledge. The model-based approach primarily utilizes a predefine deformable human model to fit the input image in line with some specific object functions. In comparison, the data-driven approach represented by deep learning has attracted more attention in recent years and has achieved the remarkable results. However, the emerging neural rendering technology might give us some new inspirations, it could integrate the model-based and data-driven approaches and bring the V-HAR to a new level. We believe this is a promising and exciting direction in which we should put more emphasis.

Printed in the United States
by Baker & Taylor Publisher Services